THE

STORY OF CAMBERLEY

1798-1987

the Victorian village that became a modern town

Gordon Wellard

SUMMARY OF INFORMATION IN CHAPTERS

LIST OF ILLUSTRATIONS

Page

LIST OF ILLUSTRATIONS Continued

ACKNOWLEDGEMENTS

Surrey Heath Museum:	Charts on Pages 15 and 28 Photographs on Pages 17, 30, 44, 46, 71, 76, 77, 82, 95
R.M.A. Sandhurst Collection:	Illustrations on Pages 12 and 17
Ordnance Survey:	Maps on Pages 99 and 122. "Reproduced from the Ordnance Survey 1940 and 1959, one inch, and the 1982, 1.50 000 maps with the permission of the Controller of Her Majesty's Stationery Office, (c) Crown Copyright".
The Tate Gallery London:	"Return from the Ride" by Charles Wellington Furse
Popperfoto:	Photograph of the Prince of Wales in 1922 on Page 98
Syndication International:	Photograph of Princess Elizabeth in A.T.S. on Page 119
G I Barnett & Son Limited:	Street Map on Page 134
Teachers Training Centre, Carwarden House:	Maps on Pages 5 and 15
Friends:	Who have lent me Photographs, Postcards or other documents reproduced in this book:

Dr J Attenborough	C Fell	D Rayfield
Mrs M Bedford	Mrs B Gladwell	R Reid
Mrs H Bulmer	J Mee	D Shepherd
R L Cracknell	B Potter	Mrs M White
E Crockford	F A G Penhallow	

Colonel Alan Shepperd and Dr T A Heathcote:	For permission to quote from their own writings about the Royal Military Academy Sandhurst, utilised by me in Chapter 3

ISBN 0 9514552 0 6

Published by Gordon Wellard, 22 Parkway, Camberley, Surrey.

AUTHOR'S FOREWORD

I think that I must like jig-saw puzzles! For anyone who sets himself the task of trying to discover something of the history of the place in which he was born soon finds out that that is what he has undertaken - a gigantic jig-saw puzzle. Piece by piece, one has to unravel the clues and put them together to form a part of the picture, join the sections up correctly and then at last the whole picture starts to emerge, so that one can then stand back and see what it has all been about.

The clues are to be found by talking to many old residents of the town and asking them what they can remember of days gone by; searching for old maps and plans of the district; reading most carefully anything that any other researcher has written about Frimley, Camberley or its neighbours; borrowing old photographs and postcards of the district; searching out the oldest Camberley houses that are still existing; scouring through many old local newspapers for reports and pictures of bygone events and people.

One clue often led to another, and one person whom I contacted often told me of another whom they thought might be able to help me in my research. In the course of this I have made many new friends and this has been a reward in itself. I totted it up the other day, and found that altogether I had contacted 54 people during the years that it has taken me to write this book, many of whom were previously unknown to me, and who, when they knew what I was endeavouring to do, gave freely of their time to see me and talk to me.

Everywhere I went, I was met with kindness and helpfulness, and this was especially so from others such as Ken Clarke, Heather Toynbee, Kitty Dancy and Colonel Alan Shepperd who have all written their own books about the District. Others I would like to mention with gratitude for their help are: Sharon Cross, the Curator of Surrey Heath Museum; Dr Heathcote, the Curator of the Sandhurst Collection; Philip Stevens, the Chairman of the Surrey Heath Local History Club; Mr Penhallow for the loan of his postcard collection; Mr Johns for his invaluable reminiscences; Dr John Attenborough for the loan of his priceless maps and books; Mr Goold of Henry Street's Nurseries for the information he gave me about Heatherside; Mr Gayler and Mr Lawson for their help with many of the illustrations; Mrs Bulmer for her help at Maywood and the two Miss Fairs for their information about Mr Doman.

I would also like to record my thanks to Tony Woodcock and Sue Roggero for the many hours that they so cheerfully spent hunting out old maps and photographs that they thought would be useful to me and photostating them at the Surrey Heath Museum, they were of great value to me.

And, above all, I owe a very special thank you to my wife, Margaret, for putting up with the inconvenience of having our Dining Room out of use for a little over a year whilst it was covered with maps, papers, books and other paraphernalia connected with my research. To say nothing of the fact that she has been a "Research Widow" for so many hours each day whilst I was miles away with my head in the clouds of Camberley's past!

I must now hope that you enjoy the book that you are about to read and find the Story of our Town as interesting as I did whilst compiling this record.

Gordon Wellard

June 1988

CHAPTER 1

By comparison with our neighbours, Bagshot and Frimley, the story of the founding and development of Camberley covers a comparatively short period of time, 185 years starting from the year 1800.

The area that we think of as Camberley extends from the Blackwater River in the west to the Maultway in the east, with the London Road as its northern boundary and the Chobham and Bisley roads as its southern boundary.

In 1800 this area was known as Frimley Heath and was practically uninhabited except for the strip of rather marshy land that lay between the river and the Frimley Road. Part of this was Bristow Farm which had existed there since 1418.

To the north and east Frimley Heath was surrounded by the Crown Lands of Windsor Forest. Hunting was the sport of kings as well as the aristocracy and landed gentry. Deer, foxes and other game abounded, indeed they are still to be found on Old Dean Common and around Heatherside. Generally this type of country was then considered to be barren waste land, and such was thought to be its value when the Army was looking for a site on which they might build an officers' military training college towards the end of the 18th century.

The story of our town's founding is almost wholly bound up with the need of the Army in the year 1800 to provide proper training facilities for its officers on a truly professional basis. The system whereby officers purchased their commissions and were then often called upon to lead their troops into battle having had little training for the job, had hitherto been the general practice. The shortcomings of this system had been shown up in the Napoleonic wars we were engaged in between 1795-1815, and the need for better training facilities for Staff Officers, again shown up as an absolute necessity by the Crimean War in 1854-56.

This led to the foundation of the Royal Military College at Sandhurst in 1812, and the Staff College at Camberley in 1862. Additionally two large Military Camps were established some five miles from the R.M.C. at North Camp and South Camp in 1854, these being sited on Aldershot Common where there were only 850 inhabitants. Why did the Army come here? To understand this, and just how and why Camberley has developed as it has today, it is necessary to study a contour map of the area extending from Wokingham in the north to Farnham in the south, bounded on the west by Hartley Wintney and in the east by Bisley.

Through 90% of this area the sluggish and far from beautiful Blackwater River flows with its offshoot, Cove Brook. The River Wey which flows eastward from Alton towards Godalming shares the same valley in which the Blackwater runs for a short stretch, the two rivers nearly meeting at Weybourne.

To the north and to the east of Blackwater valley is a high range of hills, Easthampstead Plain and Chobham Ridges, from which seven spurs of high ground extend westwards towards the river. Between these are five valleys which at one time had streams running along them.

To the south and to the west of the river are the Hartford Bridge Flats

THE BLACKWATER VALLEY IN 1816

Additions: Reading - Reigate Railway 1849. Aldershot North & South Camps 1854.
London - Southampton Railway 1838.

and an even higher range of hills, Aldershot Heights, wherein Aldershot and Farnham are situated. Between these two towns, at Ayling Hill, 550 ft above sea level the River Blackwater rises and first running eastwards and then northwards eventually flows into the Loddon at Swallowfield.

In 1800, there was a series of small farms all along the river valley with here and there a small hamlet, Eversley, Yateley, Sandhurst, Darby Green and Blackwater being numbered among them. Frimley was a little larger than these and could be called a village.

Most of these were part of the Manorial Estates which occupied the fertile strip of land on either side of the river. From the confluence of the Blackwater with the Whitewater River near Swallowfield, Bramshill Park Manor spread along the valley to Eversley Cross, where it met Yateley Manor, and then this was followed by Sandhurst Park, which reached as far as Blackwater hamlet. From here Frimley Manor occupied the eastern side of the valley, southwards to Mytchett, where the Manors of Ash, Tongham and Aldershot joined. On the western side was Frogmore Park and the Manors of Hawley and Cove.

The majority of the farmers were tenants of the Lord of the Manor, some of whom had "copyhold" rights of tenure: i.e. they held the land on certain conditions that were laid down and "copied" on the rolls of the manor. These specified duties which they had to undertake, in order to hold their land continuously, instead of holding it at the will of the lord alone. Provided these were carried out satisfactorily this enabled many families to pass their farms from father to son over long periods of time, thus creating a sort of leasehold that was combined with freehold. Some of the farmers had managed to purchase their farms and these were of course held freehold, but there were few of these.

The Manorial Estates only occupied the more fertile low-lying land along the river valley. In 1800 they did <u>not</u> own any of the higher heathland and forest land that surrounded the valley, and in particular Frimley Manor did <u>not</u> own Frimley Heath or any part of Easthampstead Plain or the Chobham Ridges. This "waste" land was Common Land that could be used by anyone at will.

Along the range of hills that lay to the north and east of the river ran an ancient sheep track called the Maultway. The whole of this area was scrubland, with sparse grass and small clumps of trees and was almost entirely uninhabited. Every year great herds of sheep were driven to market from the Berkshire Downs via Pangbourne and Wokingham and then along Easthampstead Plain and the Chobham Ridges to Tongham, where they turned westwards to cross the valley at the Weybourne gap between the rivers Blackwater and Wey. Thence their route continued just south of the Aldershot Heights to their destination of Crondall, where they hoped to sell their flocks at the great Sheep and Cattle Fair held there annually.

When the herd reached a point near Blackwater a part of it was detached to be offered for sale at Blackwater's own Sheep Fair which was held in November each year.

You may ask why these herds travelling from Wokingham to Crondall were not driven along the easy valley route instead of the more difficult one over the hills, the answer being that the farmers would not allow them to graze their sheep in their pastures en route. Instead they had to travel over what was common land, where despite the poor grass they could find some feed for their flocks, and this meant travelling along the "hills" route.

Surrey Hill, just to the north of Camberley is 427 feet above sea level and the highest point of the "Maultway" range. From a point near here the Wish Stream still flows towards the R.M.C. lakes and thence on to finish in the Blackwater and forms the boundary between Berkshire and Surrey. Similarly, the Blackwater River is the boundary between Surrey and Hampshire.

The Cam Stream can no longer be seen as it now runs underground, but back in 1816 the first Ordnance Survey map shows it as flowing to the river from a small lake located near the Frimley Road at Belmont Road. The original course of this stream ran parallel to the railway track, and started on Old Dean Common. (Map page 10)

The Watchetts Stream ran through the valley between Crawley Hill and Frimley Ridge alongside the Portsmouth Road. The upper part of this stream is now in a culvert under the M3 Motorway, but the lower part still exists above ground flowing into the Watchetts Lake and then continuing on under the Frimley Road and through the Watchmoor Industrial Estate to the river.

The Frimley Stream ran to Tomlins Pond in the valley between the Frimley Ridge and Jackpond hill, and thence to a small pond near the Frimley Cottage Hospital where it divided, half going northwards to join up with the Watchetts Stream, on the way being joined by a small stream running from the lake by the Frimley Park Manor House, and the other half ran southwards to the river.

The Middle Moor Stream ran from the valley between Frith Hill and Blackdown Hill, through Middle Moor and entered the Blackwater near where Johnsons Factory is today, passing through St. Catherines en route.

In 1816 few roads existed in Camberley. The two main roads were turnpike roads over which travellers had to pay a toll. These were the London Road and Portsmouth Road. Frimley Road connected these two, but the only other road within this triangle was a short one that connected Frimley Manor House to Hacklane Farm. From here a track went towards Crawley Hill but after 100 yards broke into three separate tracks across Frimley Heath - one to New Farm by the London Road, one to a Keeper's lodge on the Portsmouth Road, and the third along the Crawley Ridge, past a number of small gravel pits, to join up with Gibbet Lane.

Frimley was connected to Lightwater and Windlesham by the Chobham Road, and to Bisley by the Bisley Road, and these crossed the Maultway which was just a wide track. Field Lane led from Frimley to Tomlinscote but ceased there. All these roads were gravel roads and travelling over them was a very "dusty" business! A short road linking the Manor House to Bristow Farm also existed. In 1770 there had been a road connecting Blackwater to Lightwater directly across Frimley Heath via Crawley Hill, but by 1816 this had disappeared from the map. Another road existing in 1793 was King's Ride, so named because George III used to break off from the London Road at this point to ride over the moor to Windsor when returning from Exeter, and this existed in 1800, as did Gibbet Lane which was the start of a track leading to Bracknell. But that was all there was.

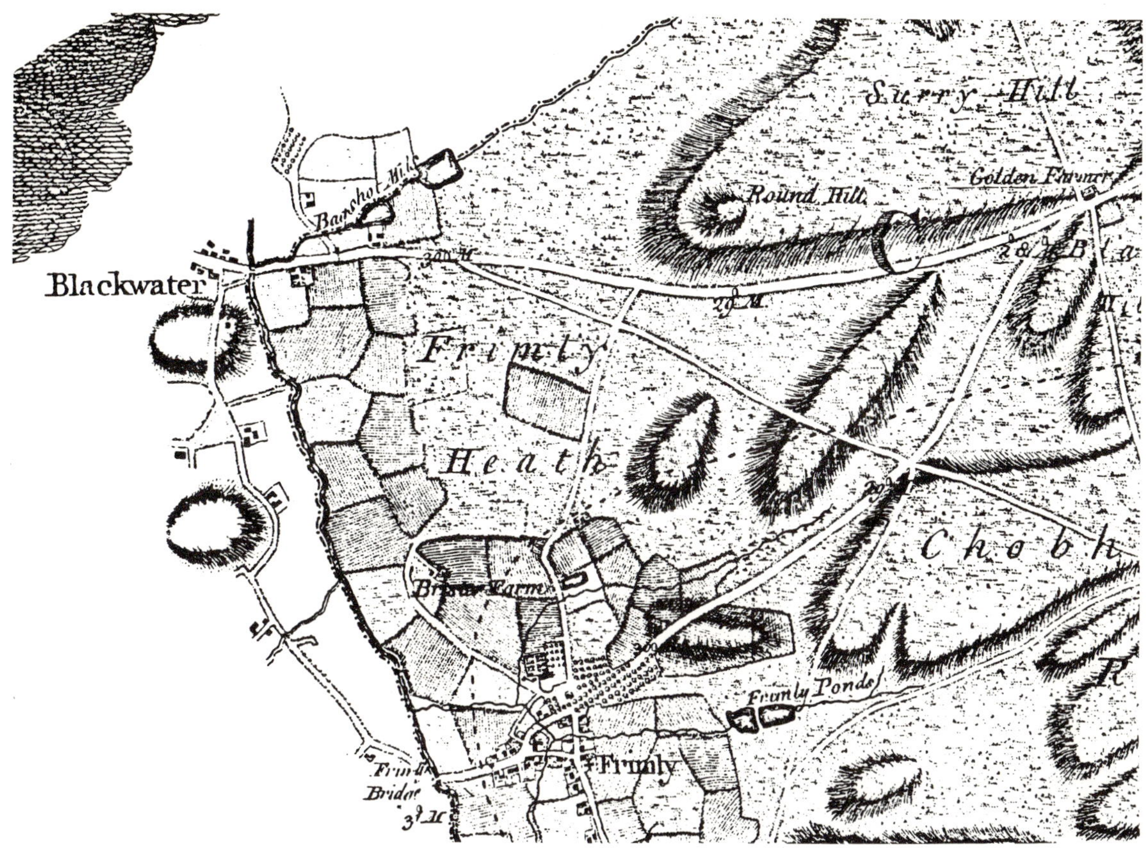

Frimley Heath 1770. At that time the only land belonging to the Lords of Frimley Manor were the fields to the left of the map. The Wish Stream (via Bagshot Mills), the Watchetts Stream and Frimley Stream are all seen running into Blackwater River.

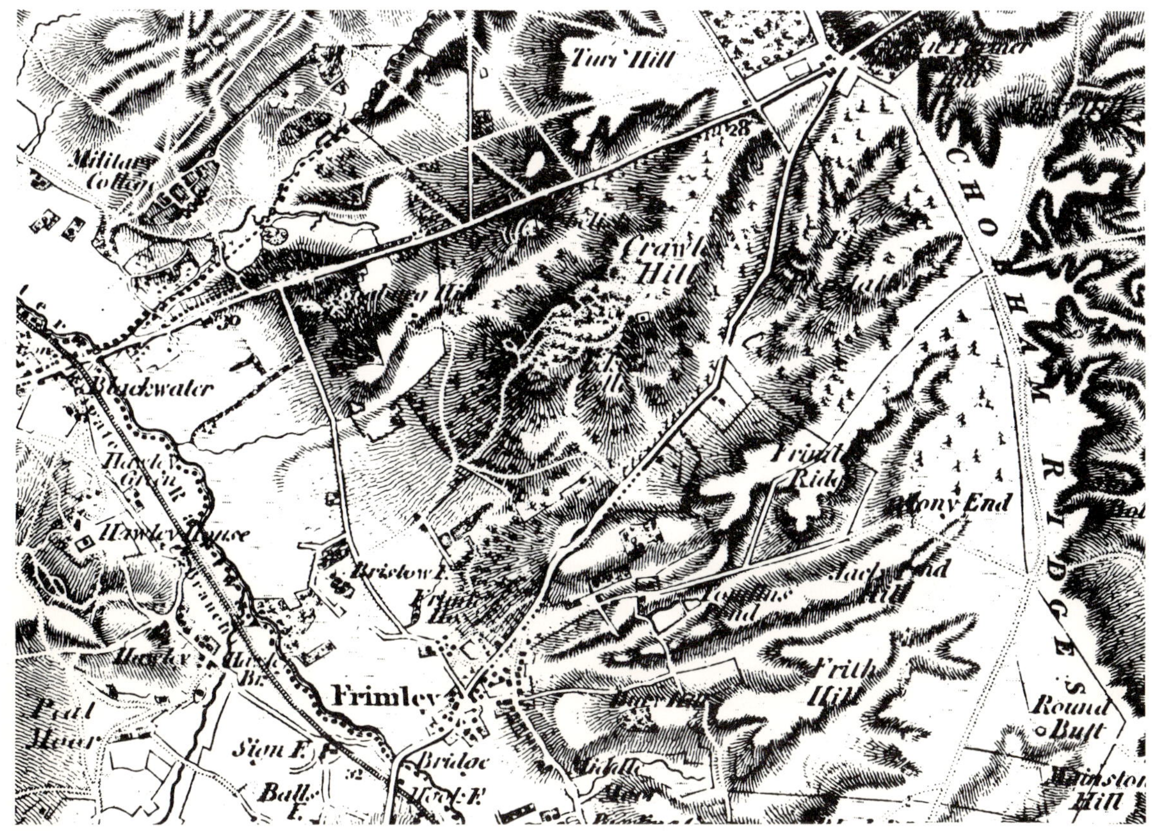

First Ordnance Survey map of Camberley. Cam Stream can be seen flowing to Blackwater River. Also tracks over Crawley Ridge. Colling Ridge is where "Fir" is on the map.

CHAPTER 2

In the year 1800, Blackwater, Frimley and Frimley Green were all part of a huge estate known as Frimley Manor. In 1537 this estate, together with other vast tracts of land, were owned by Chertsey Abbey, but the monks surrendered these to Henry VIII upon the dissolution of the monasteries and Frimley Manor became Crown Property.

In 1553 Henry's daughter, Queen Mary I, held a court at the White Hart Inn, Frimley and took over the Frimley Manor Estate. A year later she gave this, together with the Manor of Aldershot, to Sir James White, one of her courtiers, who afterwards became a Lord Mayor of London. After his death in 1573, his son Robert, who inherited the estates, added the Manor of Tongham to his possessions. He died in 1599 and left his Manors in joint possession to his twin daughters, Ellen and Mary, who had married twin brothers, Sir Richard and Sir Walter Tichborne of Tichborne Park, near Alresford, Hampshire. When Lady Ellen Tichborne died in 1606 her part of her father's estate passed to Lady Mary Tichborne who survived her. Thereafter it remained in the possession of the Tichborne family until 1789, when they sold Frimley Manor to James Laurell of Littlehampton for £20,250.

Sir James Tichborne who had the estate from 1680-1750 had nine children, the first five of whom were girls, followed by a boy who died in infancy, then another girl, and at last a boy, Henry, who survived to succeed him. In 1710 Sir James built Frimley Park Manor House, the most beautiful and gracious house in the district, on the site of an unpretentious hunting lodge that had existed there since the early 1660's. It had, and still has, beautifully laid out pleasure gardens and a delightful small lake to the rear of the house. The Tichborne family's connection with Camberley is commemorated by their arms being included in Frimley and Camberley's coat of arms and a number of their family are buried in the crypt of St.Peter's, Frimley.

James Laurell died in 1799 without making a will, but his son, another James, succeeded in laying claim to his father's estate. At that time the lands of the Manor comprised about 1,315 acres, stretching along the Blackwater Valley from Blackwater village southwards to Mytchett village. In the area between Blackwater and Frimley, the strip of farmland between the river and Frimley Road, plus the Watchetts and the Manor House with their surrounding pleasure gardens and farms, was the only part of modern Camberley that the Manor owned.

Between Frimley and Frimley Green, there were six farms, occupied by the Lord of the Manor's tenant farmers and these lay between the river and St.Catherines Road. All the land to the east of the Manor which lay towards the Maultway and the Chobham Ridges was called "waste" land. In 1801 the Frimley Enclosure Act was passed by Parliament which dealt with the disposal of this land.

Enclosure Acts had originated due to the following circumstances. In the 17th century agriculture was the chief occupation of all countrymen and up to 1650 the "Open Field" system of cultivation was in general usage, whereby grazing for sheep and cattle was held in common usage by a village community. But, during Elizabeth I's reign, the nobles, gentry and other freeholders had commenced to add to their lands and turned vast tracts into enclosed pasture for their sheep, and country labourers had been losing

Map illustrating the effect of the Frimley Enclosure Act 1801.

Original Frimley Manor Estate of James Laurell.
Area enclosed and awarded to James Laurell to increase his Manor.
Land belonging to other Freeholders.
Land enclosed and awarded to other Freeholders and Copyholders.
Poors Allotment for Fuel.
Lady Griselda Tekell's Sandhurst Park Bought for the R.M.C..
Land purchased from the Enclosure Commissioners for the R.M.C..
Land granted to the R.M.C. as a gift from the Crown.
Land outside the boudaries of the Frimley Enclosure Act.

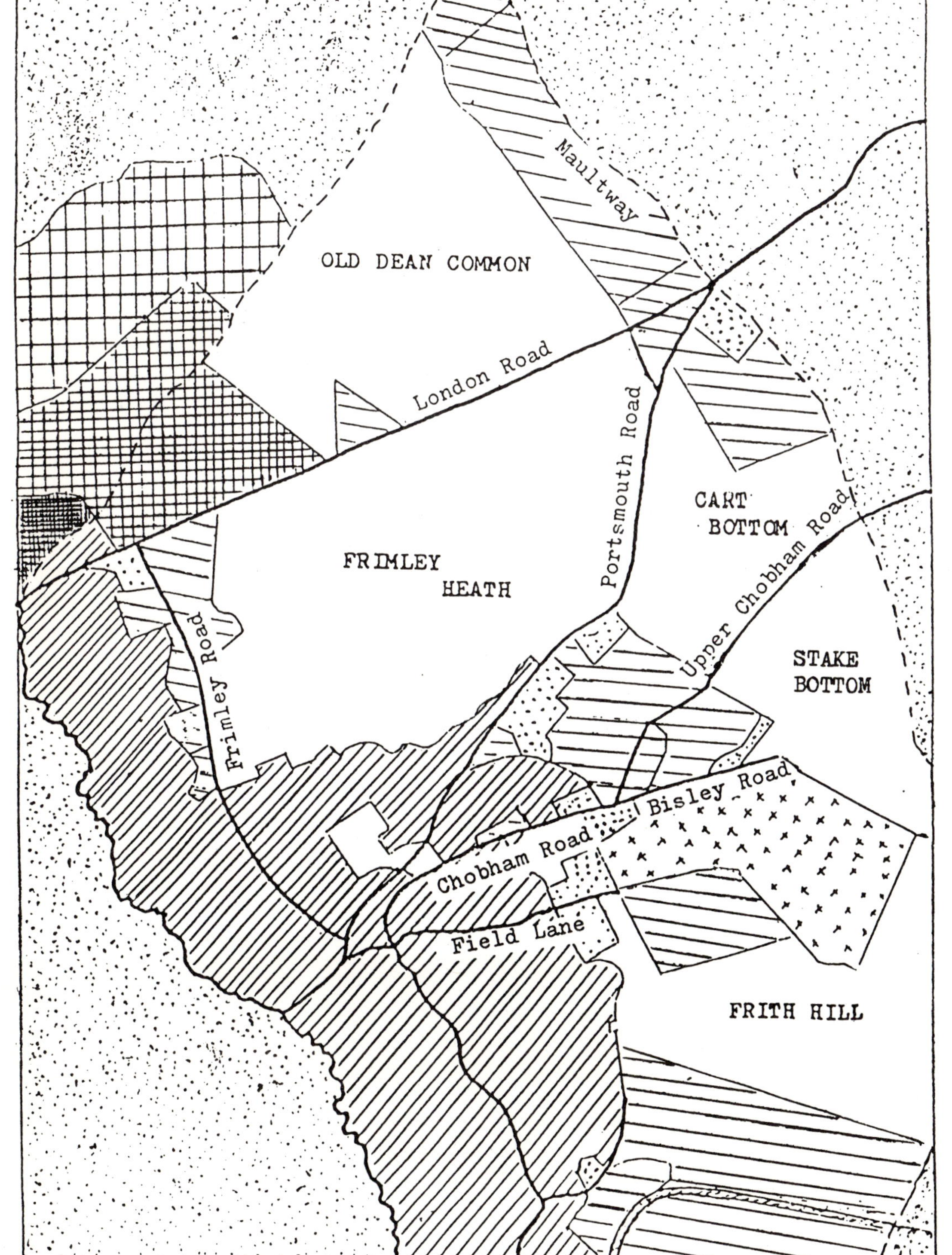

their rights to share in the use of what had hitherto been common land when it became walled in. The theory put forward to justify these enclosures was that in the process of commercialising agriculture to allow farming to be done on a much larger scale, it was thought to be the only way in which comprehensive drainage schemes etc, aimed at improving the yield of the land, could be made. By the 1750's the growth in population, together with bad harvests and wars, helped to focus the need to bring still more land under cultivation if Britain was to be able to feed her people adequately. Hence the new Enclosure Acts designed to encourage this, but alas sadly open to abuse. In George III's reign, 1,532 separate Enclosure Acts were passed, dealing with nearly 3 million acres of "waste" land.

These Acts distributed this land between the lord of the manor and various persons who claimed a right to it, which they had to establish through the court and prove their tenure of land already possessed in the area to be enclosed. In 1801 a special Act ruled that the consent of three-quarters of the freeholders and copyholders of the manor was necessary before land could be enclosed, and in 1845 the whole matter of an enclosure was put in the hands of especially appointed Commissioners whose business it was to examine a suggested enclosure and see that some part of the land was set aside for public purposes, and for the poor of the district to be able to obtain fuel from it. These became known as Fuel Allotments, and one such was established in Frimley.

The Frimley Enclosure Act gave James Laurell the opportunity to enlarge his Manor estate enormously and by dint of obtaining some land by purchase from the commissioners and some to which his tenure as Lord of the Manor entitled him, he was able to add the whole of Frimley Heath and most of the high ground of the Chobham Ridges, including Old Dean Common, to his estate, increasing it from its original 1,315 acres to 3,500 acres (i.e. from about 2 square miles to nearly 5½ square miles).

In the area of modern Camberley that lies between the London Road (A30) and the Chobham/Bisley Road comprising 4½ square miles, Laurell acquired 2¼ square miles to add to the 1 square mile he already owned. The other 1¼ square miles of "waste" land enclosed was shared among half a dozen others who were able to establish their claims to the commissioners. Amongst these were Timothy Curtis, who successfully claimed the land subsequently sold to the Royal Albert Orphanage; Thomas Thick, the publican who held the licence of the "Jolly Farmer", was awarded the Heathermount estate (part of which is now occupied by Collingwood School); Thomas Knight, was given the land on which about half of Camberley Heath Golf Course now stands, and the Hon. Alexander Murray secured the Winding Wood Road area just to the south of this. In Yorktown, Joseph Graves was awarded the Woodlands Estate lying between The Avenue and Frimley Road and some land opposite leading to the Peat Moor on which Yorktown Industrial Estate was later built. Benjamin Briggs and John Goddard were given the strip of land stretching from Vale Road to the railway bridge over the Frimley Road, now occupied by a row of houses.

Laurell also claimed, and was awarded, about ¾ square mile of land to the north of the London Road, and south of the Wish Stream, known as Old Dean Common, and Sir Timothy Curtis was also given ¼ square mile. It is on a part of this that the Old Dean housing estate now stands.

Between the Chobham/Bisley Road in Frimley and the Basingstoke Canal in Frimley Green, there is an area of approximately 2½ square miles. The Manor Estate of James Laurell already owned about half of this prior to the

Enclosure Awards. The rest of this area was "waste" land spreading over Jackpond Hill, Frith Hill and Blackdown Hill comprising $1\frac{1}{4}$ square miles and this was shared out between Laurell, $\frac{1}{2}$ square mile; tenant farmers and others, $\frac{1}{4}$ square mile; with the rest being used for a Poors Allotment of $\frac{1}{2}$ square mile for the benefit of the inhabitants of Frimley for them to be able to obtain fuel.

The 550 acre area enclosed by James Laurell junior, that lay to the east of Portsmouth Road, stretching towards Chobham Ridges, was known as Cart Bottom and Stake Bottom. Down the centre of this area was Frimley Ridge, along which Upper Chobham Road now runs. To the east of Frimley Ridge is Heatherside, and to the west Collingwood Park. I believe it got its name this way. When James Laurell inherited the Manor Estate he set about turning some of his land into profitability and this was especially true of the land he had just enclosed. In those days great landowners planted trees as a crop with the objective of producing income for their grandchildren when the trees could be harvested. The moorland area to the north of Frimley Ridge was most suitable for this and he planted some 2,000 trees here in the area between Portsmouth Road and The Maultway, which became known as Collingwood Park, no doubt because of the Wood plantation near Colling Ridge, on Black Hill, marked as "Fir Plantation" on the map on Page 5.

I have also been told that about 1850, a Dr Cuthbert Collingwood, who was a naturalist and surgeon, purchased a 100 acre estate in the north eastern part of Cart Bottom, which had not been planted with trees, with the intention of growing crops, grasses and plants there, but by 1861 he had found the ground too barren and gave up in despair. He had built a villa on this estate which he called "Collingwood Court". In 1861 he sold his estate together with his villa to the Royal Albert Orphanage Trust.

Sir Henry Tichborne, the 7th Bt., was born at Frimley in 1756 and he succeeded his father to the Baronetcy in 1785. At that time the ancestral seat of the Tichborne family, Tichborne House (depicted to the left in 1670) was in a state of disrepair and so Sir Henry decided to pull down the existing house and replace it with the house shown in the right hand picture. To help finance this he sold Frimley Manor to James Laurell for £20,250. With a part of this he purchased Sevington Manor for £3,500 which adjoined Tichborne Park and then commenced to build the new house in 1802. Soon after, when on a visit to France, he was taken prisoner at the commencement of the Napoleonic wars and was detained there until 1814, after which he returned to England to rejoin his family, who had then resided in the house for 10 years.

The present owner of Tichborne House is Mrs J.Loudon, the eldest daughter of the last baronet, Sir Anthony Tichborne.

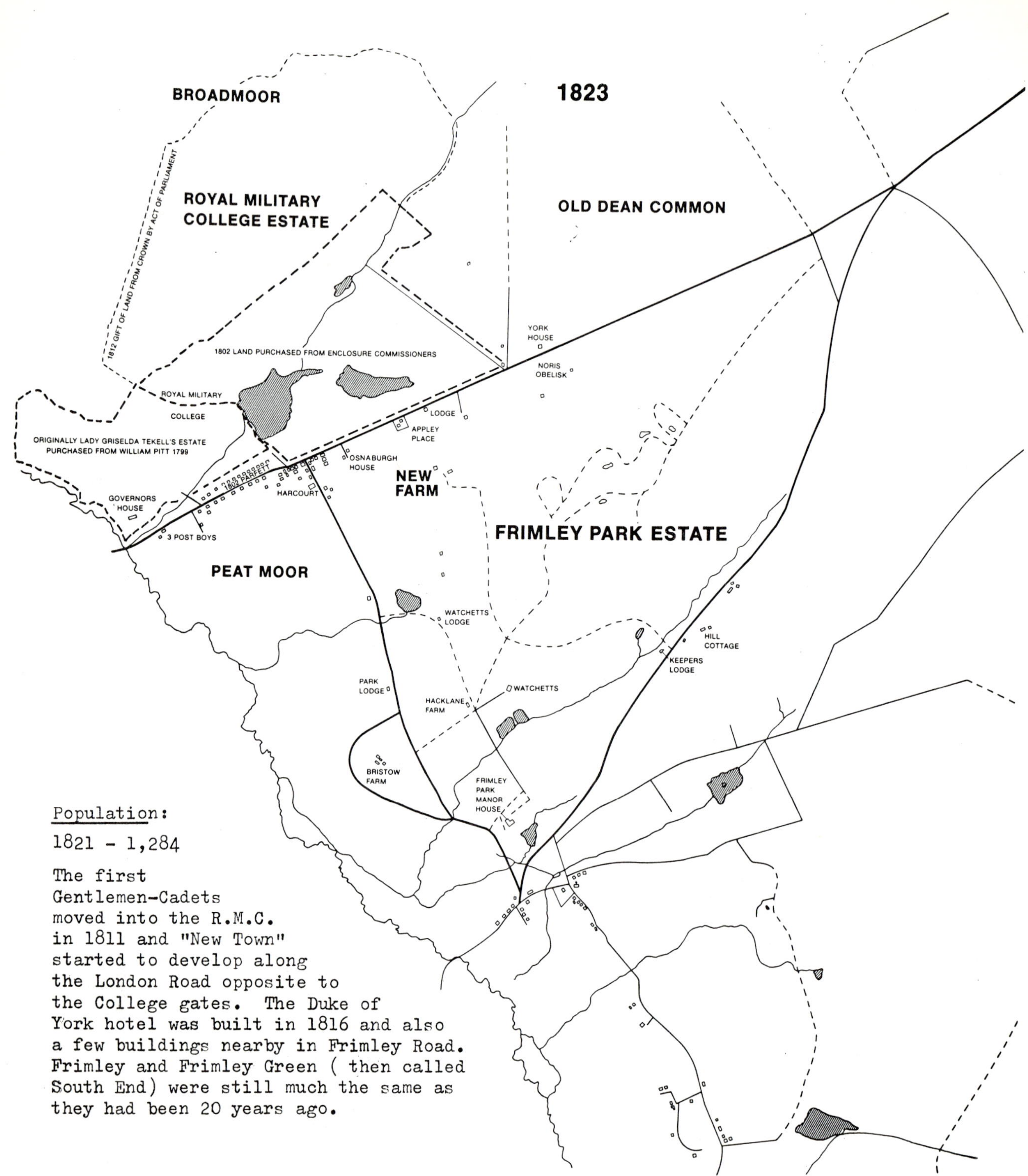

Population:

1821 - 1,284

The first Gentlemen-Cadets moved into the R.M.C. in 1811 and "New Town" started to develop along the London Road opposite to the College gates. The Duke of York hotel was built in 1816 and also a few buildings nearby in Frimley Road. Frimley and Frimley Green (then called South End) were still much the same as they had been 20 years ago.

Please note:

In order to enable an adequate comparison to be made between the population figure shown here and those on all other maps and elsewhere when quoted in this book the figure shown is that applicable to the area that became the Frimley and Camberley Urban District Council comprising Frimley,Camberley,Frimley Green and Mytchett. After 1973, when the F.& C.U.D.C. had Bagshot,Chobham,Windlesham,Bisley,West End and Lightwater added to it to become the Borough of Surrey Heath, a separate population figure is also given for the enlarged area of the Borough on the maps on Pages 117 and 129.

CHAPTER 3

By the year 1801, some developments had occurred in the area just to the east of Blackwater village. Sandhurst Park was situated there a little to the north of the London Road. It was a 450 acre estate consisting of a large red-brick house which was in a rather poor state of repair, the Park farm, and a mill worked by the Wish Stream. Its southern boundary ran along the Wish Stream from Blackwater Bridge to the Mill, by the side of which were two Mill ponds. The boundary then ran west around what are now playing fields along to the present College Town exit gate of the R.M.A.S. Sandhurst, and then across to the River Blackwater. The Park had first been owned by Richard Lodge and then by his son, Thomas, who died in 1752, both being buried at St Peters. In 1799 the assignees of Thomas Lodge sold this property to John Tekell, whose history is of particular interest to us since a part of Camberley still bears his name.

Tekell, whose home was Barningham Hall in Yorkshire, was a former lieutenant in the infantry, who having sold his commission on leaving the army, had a substantial capital sum available to invest in land deals. He obviously moved in Georgian society, for in 1800 he married Lady Griselda Stanhope, the daughter of the 3rd Earl of Stanhope. Her mother, Hester Stanhope, was the daughter of William Pitt, the 1st Earl of Chatham, and sister of Pitt the younger, the then Prime Minister. Lady Griselda was the second of three little girls, and her mother died in childbirth after being married only 6 years to Earl Stanhope. The Earl seems to have taken little interest in and had little control over his 3 daughters, though he provided them with a step-mother by his early marriage in 1781, which gave him his heir.

The eldest, Lady Hester, went to keep house for her uncle, William Pitt the Prime Minister, who never married. The youngest, Lady Lucy, who was very pretty, ran off in 1796 with Thomas Taylor, the family's medical adviser, when she was only sixteen.

At the same time, Lady Griselda left home and was lent a house at Walmer by her uncle, Pitt, on the estate which he held in his capacity as Warden of the Cinque Ports. Pitt was an indulgent uncle, and did much to help his two nephews-in-law, John Tekell and Thomas Taylor, to advance themselves and so provide for the Stanhope girls, appointing John to be Comptroller of the Mint.

Just what induced John Tekell to purchase the delapidated Sandhurst Park in 1799 is a matter of surmise. Perhaps Lady Griselda, whom he was about to marry, gave him a hint that the Government might be interested in purchasing the estate at a later date, and this caused him to invest his capital in its purchase. In 1801, whilst the newly married Tekells were living at Walmer, they sold the Sandhurst Estate to William Pitt. A few months later Pitt sold the lands to the Treasury to be used as the site for the new Royal Military College. They paid him £8,000 for the estate.

A small strip of land lay between the Wish Stream and the London Road which the Treasury wished to purchase in addition to the Park lands in order to erect houses for the college professors. Mr Parfett, who was a brewer from Eversley owned these two fields and also the nearby 3 Post Boys Inn. The London Road was a turnpike road then and a Toll Gate was situated adjacent to Laundry Lane. Mr Parfett had purchased this land in 1805 from

Major General Le Marchant. From a drawing by J.D. Harding.

Major General Le Marchant. From a drawing by J.D.Harding. The existence of the Royal Military College at Sandhurst was largely due to his inspiration.

The Sandhurst site, c. 1811, showing the progress on the College buildings and work on digging out the lake. RMA Sandhurst Collection.

The small Mill Pond on the Wish Stream was dug out and enlarged to form the Lower Lake in front of the College and the earth so removed utilised to form the parade ground in front of the Old Building.

James Laurell, and soon after sold it to the Treasury, for £1,310, who built a row of 13 houses there in 1809 which were afterwards nicknamed Tea Caddy Row by the coachmen passing by on the turnpike, and they are often still called this by their occupants today.

The Wish Stream, on its route to the Blackwater from the Mill, ran over a little waterfall and then forded the London Road before reaching the river, and the R.M.C. built a laundry here. Some 120 years later we nearly had Camberley's first and only Council-owned swimming pool constructed on this site, but at the last minute the plan was cancelled.

There were several other fields existing just south of the London Road between Frimley Road and Blackwater Bridge, and just to the south of these was a Peat Moor on which most of Yorktown Industrial Estate is now built. This moor was in all probability the northern boundary of Bristow Farm, and years later Moorlands Road and Vale Road were so-named because they led on to it. In 1819 this moorland was given to the Governors of the Bounty of Queen Anne, a church charity whose aim it was to raise funds with which to build churches in the district, and the vicar of St.Peters, Frimley, was appointed as one of the Governors.

When Parfett bought the two fields just to the south of the Wish Stream, he also bought two fields on the southern side of the London Road opposite. On this land a row of cottages and a few small villas were now built for the workmen building the College, and the civilians employed there. This was the start of "New Town". In 1802 the Treasury added to their R.M.C. land by the purchase of an area, spreading from their existing estate eastwards to Kings Ride, from the Enclosure Commissioners for £1,357, and in 1812 the R.M.C. estate was further enlarged northwards by a gift of Crown Land which at the same time extinguished commoners rights to the use of this land - this is the area north of the R.M.C. towards Wishmoor. Today the public do have access to most of this area for walks, and with its lovely heather and pines this moorland is really delightful on a summer's day. Also it shows us what the whole of the area now covered by the town and houses of Camberley must have looked like in 1812, when the R.M. College was at last occupied.

The Royal Military College owes its very existence here to Major-General Le Marchant whose family home was at Chobham. His was the guiding light behind its whole conception and it was his recommendations that formed the basis of an "Outline" studied by a special committee that was set up in 1802 by the Commander-in-Chief, the Duke of York, to make plans for the construction of a building to house the Junior Department of the R.M.C.

One of the reasons that they decided to choose Sandhurst as a suitable site for the R.M.C. was that the whole of the immediate area was thinly populated, and a barren moorland area, so that it was a "neighbourhood unlikely to be injurious to the morals of the cadets and which allows space for military movements and the construction of military works without interruption". Perhaps this explains why the R.M.C. has always kept itself somewhat aloof from the activities of the military university town of Camberley of which it is a part! Today few of its inhabitants have ever set foot in its ground or seen any of its fine buildings except in pictures on their T.V. screens.

Between the years 1802-1808 little was done towards the building of the R.M.C. During this period a Mr Bracebridge had been appointed to lay out the almost tree-less grounds and James Wyatt appointed as architect for the buildings. Some workmen's cottages were set up, and some bricks made on the site by a Mr Copeland, the contractor appointed to erect the buildings. But delay after delay occurred, due to the Treasury's inability to make up its mind what it wanted, and it was not until 1808 that at last work on digging the foundations of Old College was commenced, the building being partially occupied in 1811 and not completed until 1818.

Meanwhile a nearby militia regiment was brought in to dig out and enlarge the small mill pond by the Wish Stream to form the Lower Lake, the earth removed being utilised to make the parade ground in front of Old College. A barracks was found for these men in the old red-brick manor house that was afterwards altered and re-built into the Regency building that is now Government House. This refurbishment was done at the high cost of £3,970, to make it a suitable residence for the College Governor.

During the early summer of 1811 Le Marchant visited Sandhurst to see the progress of the work and remarked to his son Dennis, "that he felt his struggles to get the College on a proper footing would now be at an end and that it was here at Sandhurst that he could expect to pass the remainder of his days". But this was not to be, for shortly after this, he was promoted Major-General and sent to join Wellington in Spain and a year later killed at the battle of Salamanca. There is a memorial to him in St Paul's cathedral, but his true memorial is the very existence of the College which came into being due to his inspiration and dedicated efforts.

Outstanding construction work on the estate, which included building Tea Caddy Row's 13 double houses at a cost of £42,258, continued on until 1817 when Wyatt presented his bill for the buildings and the fencing of the estate. His final account being for £370,000. Additional fencing was later erected along the London Road, being thought necessary to protect the cadets from contact with a cholera epidemic then prevalent in the country, and the West Lodge was built at the same time.

The first royal visit occurred soon after the R.M.C. was first occupied, when Queen Charlotte presented colours in 1813. Her Majesty was accompanied by the Prince Regent, the Duke of York, the Duke of Clarence, the Prince of Orange and the Duke of Brunswick. In 1814, at the conclusion of the Napoleonic War, the College was inspected by the Prince Regent, accompanied by the Emperor of Russia, the King of Prussia, General Count Platos and General Bulow. The next royal visit to Sandhurst was made by King William IV in 1835, and considerable efforts were made to enable a large assembly of spectators to view the spectacle and to be able to see their King, and to witness the full ceremonial of the occasion, but our local population at that time was only about 1,450. When the building of the R.M.C. first started it had been about 500. Since then many of our Kings and Queens have taken the salute at these parades, and this year Princess Diana, the Princess of Wales, did so when not only young men, but women cadets of the W.R.A.C., were on parade. Amongst them were the daughter of King Hussein of Jordan and the son of ex-King Constantine of Greece, both of whom were present as was the Queen of Spain, Constantine's sister.

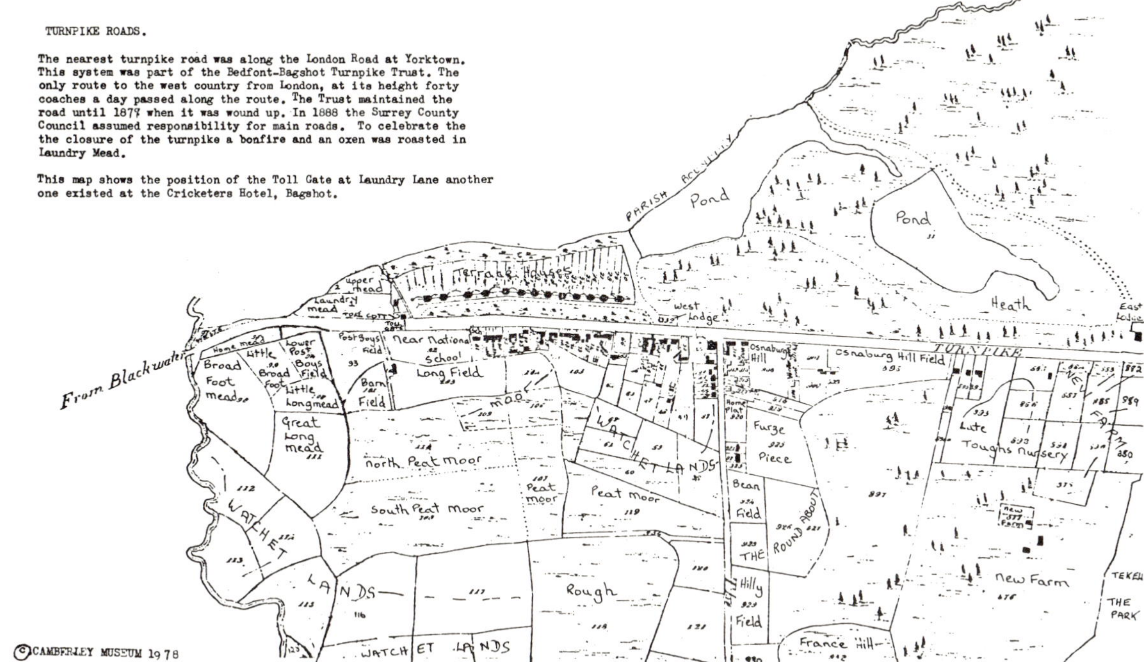

TURNPIKE ROADS.

The nearest turnpike road was along the London Road at Yorktown. This system was part of the Bedfont-Bagshot Turnpike Trust. The only route to the west country from London, at its height forty coaches a day passed along the route. The Trust maintained the road until 1877 when it was wound up. In 1888 the Surrey County Council assumed responsibility for main roads. To celebrate the the closure of the turnpike a bonfire and an oxen was roasted in Laundry Mead.

This map shows the position of the Toll Gate at Laundry Lane another one existed at the Cricketers Hotel, Bagshot.

1823. Early developments in "New Town". Tough's Nursery and New Farm to the right of the map. The beginning of Park Street which led to it can be seen in the bottom picture. Houses then existing in Frimley Green are also visible.

CHAPTER 4

The 1823 "Greenwood" map allows us to see what had occurred towards our town's development in the 10 years following the opening of the R.M.C. Change took place on the opposite side of the London Road to the College to form what was at first called "New Town", later re-named Yorktown in 1831. On the corner of the Frimley Road, Mr Parfett built the Duke of York Hotel in 1816. The old miller's house in the London Road became the Crown Inn and already existing was the Three Postboys Inn, all most conveniently placed near to the Toll Gate on the turnpike, along which some forty coaches passed each day on their route from London to the west country. The gate on the turnpike existed until 1877, when Yorktown's inhabitants celebrated its closure by roasting an oxen on Laundry Mead.

Opposite the third house in Tea Caddy Row, (where the Trend warehouse is now) the first "National School" was built. Next to this a small row of three semi-detached villas, one of which, Albany Place, was occupied by Mr Sullivan, the bandmaster at the College, who often used to play the organ at St Michaels (which was built in 1851 on land presented by the R.M.C.). He was the father of Sir Arthur Sullivan of "Gilbert and Sullivan" opera fame, and there is a small plaque on the wall of this house to commemorate the fact. Nearby is a large timbered building, now called the Agincourt Hall, and for many years this was where public meetings were held before the Civic Hall was built in 1966. Nearby were the workmen's cottages erected for Mr Copelands' men, some now converted into shops for tradesmen serving the College, of which Mr Stallwood, a bootmaker who had followed the old Military Academy from Marlow, was one. There were also a few shops close to the Duke of York Hotel in the Frimley Road.

Frimley Park Manor House was occupied by James Laurell Jnr. and it would appear that it was about this time that Watchetts House was built and the adjacent fields on the opposite side of Frimley Road to Bristow Farm turned into another farm, Axe Lane Farm, later re-named Hacklane Farm.

The land opposite to the Manor House, across the Frimley Road, was Park Farm, the home farm of the lord of Frimley Manor. Another farm was started adjacent to the London Road called New Farm, the farmhouse being situated where Firwood House was built at a later date, and it encompassed the area now bounded by Park Street and The Avenue running south to the railway. This farm later became the France Hill Estate. A track led to it over the hills from Hacklane Farm, and a short road leading to it from the turnpike was the early beginning of Park Street.

Before Laurell started to plant firs on Frimley Heath, there were some deciduous trees there interspersed with a few holly and yew trees, but it was a barren land with gorse and scrub. Later it became a deer park, with keepers' cottages on Crawley Hill and Heatherside, and also one on Portsmouth Road, Hill Cottage.

That much hunting was done was evidenced by the Obelisk, which was lit at night, and by a large lantern on Bramshill roof (now the Police College) as guides to the hunters in winter. The Obelisk, a Camberley landmark, was built by Squire Norris of Hawley around 1750 (near Knoll Road), but came to grief about 1882 when the upper part of it was burnt and later demolished, so that now only a shell remains. It originally had a gallery at the top of the walls and was crowned with a large ball. The Bramshill estate encompassed all of Eversley and extended as far as Yateley.

In Frimley village, there were a few shops in the High Street, the ancient White Hart Inn, and of course St.Peters Church, both of which date back to the 17th century. Along the road leading to Frimley Green were a number of small farms, Newbarn, Bowling Green Farm, Manor Farm, Middle Farm and Cross Farm, occupied by the tenant farmers of the Lord of the Manor.

The first church to appear in Camberley was the Baptist Chapel in Frimley Road, built close to the Duke of York hotel in 1819. This follows the pattern that I am sure many of my readers will have observed in many villages throughout the country, where the church and the village inn are close together!

The Obelisk about 1865. The wild heathland that surrounded it can clearly be seen. The picture is taken from the A30.

"Tea Caddy" Row. The houses built to accommodate the College Professors in 1813.

The Terrace or 'Tea Caddy Row', a view from the York Town Gate. RMA Sandhurst Collection.

CHAPTER 5

Just how or when John Tekell acquired the Frimley Park Estate from James Laurell junior it has been difficult to establish - a certainly known fact is that he was installed in the Manor House about 1837.

According to accounts originating with Mr G.B.Poulter's excellent "History of Camberley" written in 1937, Mr Laurell junior is supposed to have lost the whole of Frimley Park Estate in a game of cards at which the Prince Regent (later George IV) was present. This story has been repeated by other historians since, with the addition that either John Tekell won it from him or that it was sold to him in 1837.

I found the source of this story in an article "Reminiscences of Old Sandhurst" in a 1925 volume of the R.M.C. Magazine & Record in the R.M.A. Sandhurst library. This is it:

"By courtesy of Mr T.Stallwood we have been able to see some manuscript notes written by one who was a sergeant at the R.M.C. round about 1840. The notes which are undated and unsigned must have been written many years later and as they deal with the period 1825-40 are probably hearsay. Our memorist writes:-"

> "About 1837 a great stir took place in Frimley, and came on very suddenly, no notice or intention having been previously given. Squire Tekell, after 20 to 30 years exile, made his appearance with his lawyer and served a notice of 24 hours to Squire Laurell to quit and give up possession of the property where he was residing to Squire Tekell, whose it was, he (Squire Laurell) holding it as a gambling debt which he (Squire Tekell) had lost to him when the Prince of Wales was his guest at Frimley."

Another account written by Captain Kempthorne, R.A. Medical Corps, states that the Tekell family acquired the Manor of Frimley in 1799 by purchase from Mr James Laurell.

What is an absolute fact is that in 1831 the land adjacent to the R.M.C. at Barossa was in the possession of Mr Laurell since a map drawn by G.A. Barr when surveying the entire R.M.C estate names him as the occupant of the land at Barossa abutting the eastern border of the estate. This map is in the R.M.A. Sandhurst museum. It is also a fact that, in 1812 John Tekell owned the land on which our old London Road Municipal offices were built when he granted John Tough a 1,000 year lease on this land, and that Tekell's signature was appended in 1813 among other principal beneficiaries to the Frimley Enclosure Award of 1801. For a long time this was the only evidence that I could find as to the ownership of Frimley Park at that period.

Two different theories can be drawn from these accounts. The first being that Tekell bought the whole estate from Laurell soon after he had inherited it from his father in 1799. At some time between 1812-20 they played cards together (certainly before 1820 as the Prince of Wales became King then), and Tekell lost possession of the Manor to Laurell for a specified number of years, which terminated in 1837. He then arrived to claim back the Manor, but Laurell refused to quit, and so Tekell had to return with his lawyer to force him to do so. The alternative theory is that Tekell won the estate from Laurell about the year 1800, but allowed Laurell to retain possession whilst Tekell did not wish to reside in Frimley. (He had a house at Walmer). When eventually Tekell did want to reside at Frimley, Laurell would not quit without being forced to do so.

I thought the second theory to be the most likely one as it never seemed to me that Tekell could have had enough money to buy the Frimley Park Estate. He could not have received enough from the sale of his lieutenant's commission, (probably about £2,000) to have done more than buy the delapidated Sandhurst Park estate, and even if Pitt had shared some of the profit he made on selling the estate to the Treasury (after having bought it from Tekell for £3,000) Tekell would not have had the £20,000 or more that certainly would have been the price at which Frimley Park Manor Estate would have been offered for sale.

At last, in the County Records Office at Kingston, I found documents that gave me the answer to the whole mystery!

I found that James Laurell <u>sold</u> that part of his Manor Estate which lay between the London Road and the Portsmouth Road, which he now called the Frimley Park Estate, and which included the Manor House, to John Tekell on 24th March 1806 for £22,000, and that Tekell was able to make a "down" payment of £7,000 then, leaving £15,000 owing, which he then endeavoured to pay off by obtaining money bit by bit from his various friends, mortgaging to them portions of the estate as security for their loans. Meanwhile, Laurell remained in possession of the Manor House until Tekell finally managed to clear all his debts in 1837. James Laurell then went to live at Eastwick Park, Bookham, Surrey.

John Tekell's signature appears on the 1801 Enclosure award because these awards were not finally fixed until 1813, by which time Tekell as well as Laurell were among the large landowners in the area affected by it, who all then had to sign the document that set out the Commissioners' decisions.

The Tekells lived in the Manor House after coming to Frimley in 1837. The house that was to become known as "Tekells Castle" when it was built by the next owner of the estate, was only a very small hunting lodge during John Tekell's lifetime. It was situated in a fine position on Crawley Hill from which there was a splendid view over the Frimley Ridge towards Chobham Ridges, and was probably used occasionally by Lady Griselda as a summer house. After she died, in 1851, John Tekell only used it as a shooting box after a day's hunting with his friends on the estate or in the nearby Windsor forest lands.

John Tekell died in 1858, and was buried in his wife's tomb at St.Peters churchyard in Frimley. They had no children and therefore, after his death, his executors decided to sell the estate. An announcement was made in "The Times" on 12th March 1859. This read: (in brackets I have defined the places to which I think the description applies, and it is clear that the hunting lodge was not of sufficient size to warrant a special description) -

The Frimley Park Estate

A residential property with a domain of 1,457 acres ($2\frac{1}{4}$ square miles)
Presenting fine sporting features in a most excellent neighbourhood, within 2 miles of Farnborough station on the S.

Western Railway, connected with the Great Western & Brighton lines by the Reigate and Reading Railway and about one hour's journey from London.

Messrs. Daniel Smith & Son & Oakley have received instructions from the executors of the late John Tekell Esq. to submit to Public Competition at the Mart near the Bank of England in May next the above very important family mansion: (Frimley Park Manor House) containing:

17 good bedrooms and all the requisite domestic offices.
An excellent garden walled on every side, lawns and pleasure gardens adorned with silver firs of magnificent growth, ornamental water (The Lake) with gravelled walks entirely secluded by shrubberies

and

Thriving plantations of larch and Scotch fir and)
paddocks bounded by the river Blackwater interspersed) Bristow
with woodland and plantation forming excellent) and
covers admirably suited for the preservation of game) Park Farms
and intersected by little streams,)
extensive ponds well stocked with fish and (Watchetts Lakes)
the resort of wild fowl.

Also

A large tract of land with valuable plantations belted by Scots firs of large size giving the estate some very beautiful features (Tekells Park) embracing within a ring fence 1,457 acres ($2\frac{1}{4}$ square miles) bounded by capital roads (ie. London Road and Portsmouth Road) in a sporting district within easy reach of several packs of hounds in a neighbourhood affording excellent society.

The whole of the agricultural lands are in hand (Hacklane Farm, Bristow Farm, Park Farm, The Watchetts, Warren Farm and New Farm) and with a trifling exception possession may be had of the entire estate which is highly improvable and capable of development and the comfortable yet inexpensive character of the mansion, the fine and sporting features in the midst of a favourite locality, joined to an excellent railway communication render it a most valuable and desirable property.

....

The railways referred to are the London - Southampton line running through Farnborough station which was opened in 1838, and the Reading - Reigate line running through Blackwater opened in 1849.

No doubt all those who were interested in attending the forthcoming auction of this estate came down to look over the property before the sale took place in 1860. They will have noted the agent's remark that the entire estate was "highly improvable and capable of development", and that the plans were on display at the White Hart, Frimley. It is, therefore, most probable that the sale notice attracted people who may not have been looking for a lovely country estate which they themselves intended to live in and enjoy, as had been the case with its previous owners, but instead land-speculators looking for a good commercial proposition. What then was the situation that they found?

The most attractive factor was of course the forthcoming arrival of the new Staff College, the building of which had just commenced on a site to the north of the London Road near to Kings Ride.

In 1799 a military school for the professional training of officers in the more advanced aspects of war was opened at High Wycombe. In 1802 this became the Senior Department of the Royal Military College consequent upon the founding of a Junior Department at Great Marlow for the training of gentlemen-cadets. In 1812 the Junior Department moved to Sandhurst into the Old College building just completed, and the Senior Department moved to Farnham.

In 1856 the Duke of Cambridge was appointed Commander-in-Chief of the British Army at the end of the Crimean War, and the lessons learned from this war brought changes. In 1858 the Senior Department was set up in its own right as the "Staff College". New regulations were laid down for a 2 year course with proper entrance and final examinations, and a new building sought to house the College. Plans were submitted by James Pennethorne for the college to be built in the grounds of the R.M.C. at Camberley, and approved by Queen Victoria and Prince Albert who visited the site and planted a beech tree on the front lawn in 1860, and eventually the Staff College, Camberley, was opened in 1862.

Sad to say, it was only a year before this that Prince Albert contracted typhoid after one of his visits of inspection whilst the college was building, from which he died soon after. The Royal Albert Orphanage was founded in 1864 as a memorial to him, after an appeal for funds from the public had raised enough money, and this was built on the eastern part of Collingwood Park, adjacent to the Maultway.

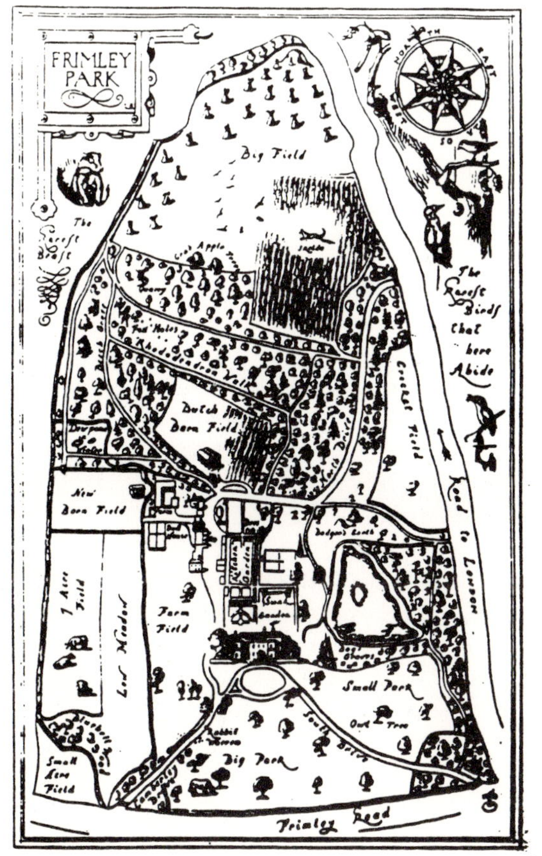

Map of Frimley Park Manor House and the pleasure gardens that surrounded it in 1880.

Frimley Park Hospital now occupies the site marked as Dutch Barn Field and Rhododendron Walk, and the hospital car park is on the Cricket Field.

Frimley Park Manor House. Built circa 1710 by Sir James Tichborne.

The Staff College,
Camberley.
Completed in 1862.

CHAPTER 6

The public auction of John Tekell's estate did not take place in May 1860, for on 3rd February his executors sold the whole 1,457 acres by private treaty to Edwin Newman of Yeovil for £32,500. This comprised the area bounded by the London Road, Gibbett Lane, Portsmouth Road and the Blackwater River.

Shortly after, on 29th June, Mr.Newman re-sold it to to Captain C.Raleigh Knight of Hersham Place, Esher, and his brother-in-law Major R.Spring of West Moulsey, Surrey. I have not been able to ascertain the amount that these gentlemen paid for the estate, but only that Captain Knight was the senior partner in the venture and did most of the financing. He was a man of great vision, energy and drive, and in the next ten years he laid the foundation upon which modern Camberley has been built. Without any doubt, he was the real founder of our town.

They divided the estate into two parts. Captain Knight took the Manor House and Park Farm opposite, and all the heathland to the east of a line drawn from Park Street to the Watchetts Lakes, and Major Spring the Watchetts Lands and Bristow Farm that lay to the west of this line, and which also included Hacklane Farm. But it is clear that the two worked in unison to develop their adjoining properties. (Maps, Page 28 and Page 29)

A delightful description of life "in service" with Captain Knight's family, which gives an insight into the type of people they were, is given in Daisy Hill's book "Old Frimley". Her grandfather was made Captain Knight's Resident Manager of the estate, and had much to do with the developments that Captain Knight undertook within the next few years. Land was cheap in those days, wages were low and there was a plentiful supply of men to labour. Moreover, he could make land developments without having to first obtain permission to do so from any form of bureaucracy.

The main factor that the brothers-in-law took into account whilst making their first plans was, of course, the building of the Staff College during the period 1859-62. Just as the R.M.C's proximity had instigated the development of Yorktown, so Captain Knight foresaw opportunities for similar developments close to the Staff College.

In Yorktown, the Duke of York hotel had been built offering accommodation to the relatives of the Gentlemen-Cadets when visiting their sons at Sandhurst, so Captain Knight thought that in Cambridge Town there was the need for a similar hotel with shops nearby to serve Staff College officers and their relatives.

Almost as soon as he got possession of the estate he started to build the Cambridge Hotel at the end of a muddy lane that went through some farm fields. This was to become the High Street, and the hotel was completed and opened in 1862. The first part of Park Street extending as far as the Carpenters Arms (built 1863) already existed as it was the road that led to New Farm. Knight now extended this towards Tekells Park and along its eastern side built Bank's cottages, a row of small cottages in which people employed in the Staff College were able to find rental accommodation. He also built a few more in two streets that he constructed joining Park Street with High Street, these being Obelisk Street and Princess Street and a few villas were built on the western side of High Street, the eastern side of

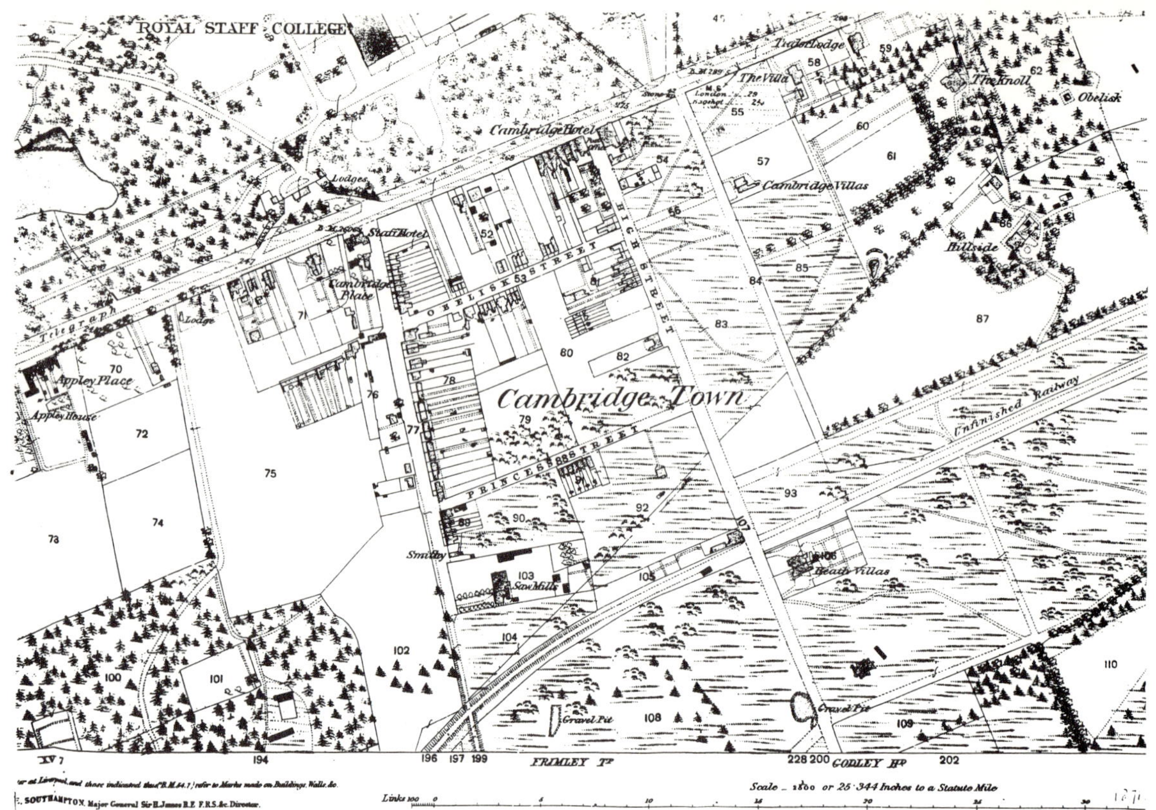

Cambridge Town 1871. High Street and Knoll Road have been cut through boggy heathland farmed by the owner of The Knoll House. The fields to the left of Park Street are New Farm. The cottages along Park Street are Bank's Cottages. The Unfinished Railway track is near Portesbery Road.

The Cambridge Hotel, the first building built in High Street by Captain R Knight in 1862. A celebration was held here in 1864 when the first turves of the Railway Track were cut.

which was still pasture.

In 1863 Captain Knight moved from Esher to take up residence in the new house he had been building on the site of Tekell's old hunting lodge. The exterior was built to resemble a small castle, as were many other Victorian mansions belonging to very wealthy men of that period, and Knight named his house "Tekells Castle". It was of a considerable size with handsome reception rooms on the ground floor and 12 bedrooms and children's nurseries on the upper floor. The outbuildings included stabling for 12 horses, coachmen's houses and entrance lodges to the estate. In front of, and surrounding the house, he laid out some beautiful gardens and below these open parkland led down to a wooded coppice that bordered the Portsmouth Road. Meantime in 1863, he sold the Manor House with its pleasure gardens and a few fields nearby (on which our Frimley Park Hospital now stands) to Mr William Stansfield. He then rented these farm fields back from him to add to his Tekell's Park farmlands. (Plan, Page 21 and Photograph of Tekells Castle, Page 33)

By this time another major factor had arisen that the brothers-in-law had to consider in formulating further plans for the development of their estates. This was the projected construction of a railway line linking the new settlements of Yorktown and Cambridge Town, as it was now called, to Sunningdale via Bagshot. In 1863, The Sunningdale and Cambridge Town Railway Company was formed and, after much discussion, a route agreed upon starting from the Frimley Road and thence via the bed of the now underground Cam Stream to Colling Ridge and so on to Bagshot. In 1864 an Act of Parliament was obtained to authorise its construction. The first turves were cut on its route through Cambridge Town in that year, after which all concerned in the ceremony repaired to the new Cambridge Hotel to celebrate the occasion by a "dejeuner". The construction of this railway continued on through 1865, but in 1866 work stopped near to the Crawley Ridge cutting, as the company ran out of funds, and it lay unfinished until 1873 when the London & South Western Company took over and extended its route southwards from Yorktown to Frimley Green and Ash Vale, completing this by 1878, and its extension from Sunningdale to Ascot in 1879.

The partners' next move was to construct a road some 100 yards to the south of the railway track to enclose the parkland part of their two estates; this became Park Road. Through the centre of their Park ran Crawley Ridge, extending from Gibbet Lane south westwards towards Hacklane Farm. This whole area was heather-clad moorland with bracken and pine trees abounding, similar to the Old Dean Common. (Photograph, Page 64)

The lower-lying land to the north of the railway contained a few hilly areas, France Hill, along which The Avenue runs today; Osnaburgh Hill on which St. Michaels was built; and the hilly area to the east of High Street alongside the London Road. As Park Road continued its route eastwards from the Frimley Road,it bent towards the railway track, which it crossed over a bridge constructed at the commencement of the Crawley Ridge cutting. From here two further branch roads connected it to the London Road. The first of these was well-named Knightsbridge Road and the other, named after the vicar of St.Michaels, Middleton Road. (Map, Page 29 and Street Map, Page 134)

The decision was then made to divide the parkland into three parts by constructing a road connecting Park Road to Portsmouth Road via Crawley Hill (Church Hill/Crawley Hill Roads), and another one from the top of Crawley Hill along the ancient track leading to Gibbet Lane (Crawley Ridge Road). The total parkland area enclosed by Park Road comprised some 850 acres of which 2/3rds was south of the Church Hill/Crawley Hill Roads, and 1/3rd to the north.

Up until 1868 no further attempt was made to develop this parkland and Captain Knight's efforts were all concentrated on the area north of Park Road. The High Street was continued onwards to join Park Road, the part south of the railway being named Heathcote Road, where he built two houses with the intention of letting them furnished. The first of these was "Heathcote House" and the other "Roydon Lodge", situated close to one of the entrance drives to his Tekells Castle Estate. Some years later, "Roydon Lodge" was occupied by General Abbot Anderson, a man who was well-loved in Camberley for his interest and benefactions to the townsfolk. When he died in 1903, a sum of money was raised by public subscription in order to erect a drinking-fountain as a memorial to him, and this was placed on the London Road Recreation Ground close to the A30, but has now been re-sited by the Arena Leisure Centre.

Captain Knight then built "Heath Villas" in Heathcote Road, also for letting, situated near to the railway track. "Camberley Towers", a block of flats, now occupies the site of these villas.

The map of Cambridge Town in 1871 shows that by then a second house had been built on the eastern side of the High Street about 20 yards away from the Cambridge Hotel. This is now called "The Crockery Shop". Almost opposite to this was the house in which I was born. In 1871 it was a semi-detached dwelling house with a cottage behind, the lower part of which was a stable, but by 1909, when it became my father's ladies hairdressers shop, the lower floor had been converted into a shop with a flat over the business premises. (It is now "Bojangles Health and Exercise Centre").

Next to this, towards Obelisk Street, was a small Nursery Garden with a large Georgian-type house beyond belonging to the owner, Mr Craig of Barossa Farm. Around 1900 this house was known as the "Lords House", as it was then occupied by a lady who ran it as a boarding house for a number of aristocratic young gentlemen who were attending Colonel Fox's "Cramming School" in nearby Knoll Road, thereby hoping to attain sufficient knowledge to enable them to pass the entrance examination into the R.M.C. Sandhurst. About 1910, Mr James Page bought this house which lay back about 10 yards from the High Street, added some shop fronts to it and turned the whole building into Camberley's first department store. Still later Mr Page's store was demolished and "Allders" store built in its place.

Continuing down the High Street, from the Obelisk Street corner, a villa and a row of five semi-detached houses all with gardens in the rear, followed. Then there was a gap of about 30 yards, and finally a house all on its own. When Mr Page first came to Camberley in about 1900, he started in business as a draper there. In 1910 this house was converted into Camberley's first cinema called "The Electric" when Mr Page moved into his new premises further up the street. There were no other buildings in the High Street in 1871, and at that time none had as yet been converted into shops.

In 1874 the first Cambridge Town shops opened in the London Road opposite to the Staff College. They had originally been built as a row of one-storied cottages, but now had shop fronts added to them. The one on the corner of the High Street became our first Post Office, which was moved a little further away in 1877, when Cambridge Town was re-named Camberley to avoid postal confusion with Cambridge in East Anglia. The next two cottages were demolished about 1900, and the graceful, half-timbered building that is still in existence there took their place. At first this was occupied by Mr Close, a solicitor, and Mr Poulter, an architect, but later this building was turned into "Betty Browns", a delightful tea shop run by the two Miss Lindley sisters. When they retired, Mr Milner, a Yorkshireman, took over, providing a splendid 3 course lunch for 1/6d, as well as teas. It is still being utilised as a restaurant at the present time, but sadly threatened by a new scheme to re-develop this area.

Two of the other cottages became Verrans, a butchers, and Andrews, a haberdashers. Next to these, and the first shop to open there, was "Pank's Emporium", a wonderful old ironmongers and hardware shop that had brooms, brushes and buckets hanging from the ceiling, and was absolutely crammed to the doors with every conceivable sort of dish or household utensil one could think of. Mr Pank was a dear old man, the landlord of my father's shop in High Street, and when I was a little boy he always treated me very kindly, as did the occupant of the shop opposite to us.

This was owned by Mr Percy J.Todd, a watchmaker and jeweller, who was a superb model-maker. He made a marvellous working model of a "merry-go-round" roundabout which was composed of 3,000 parts, complete with a tiny organ that played six tunes, which he copied from a showman's model, probably from one in Whittles Fair who used to park their vehicles in the winter on the fields at Blackwater. He used to let me sit in his shop, where he kept his model, and then play the tunes whilst to my delight the horses went round and round in front of my large, round, little boy's eyes. I have a picture of Mr Todd with his model which appeared in the national press paper, the Sunday Pictorial, when he exhibited it in London at the Model Making Exhibition in the 1920's.

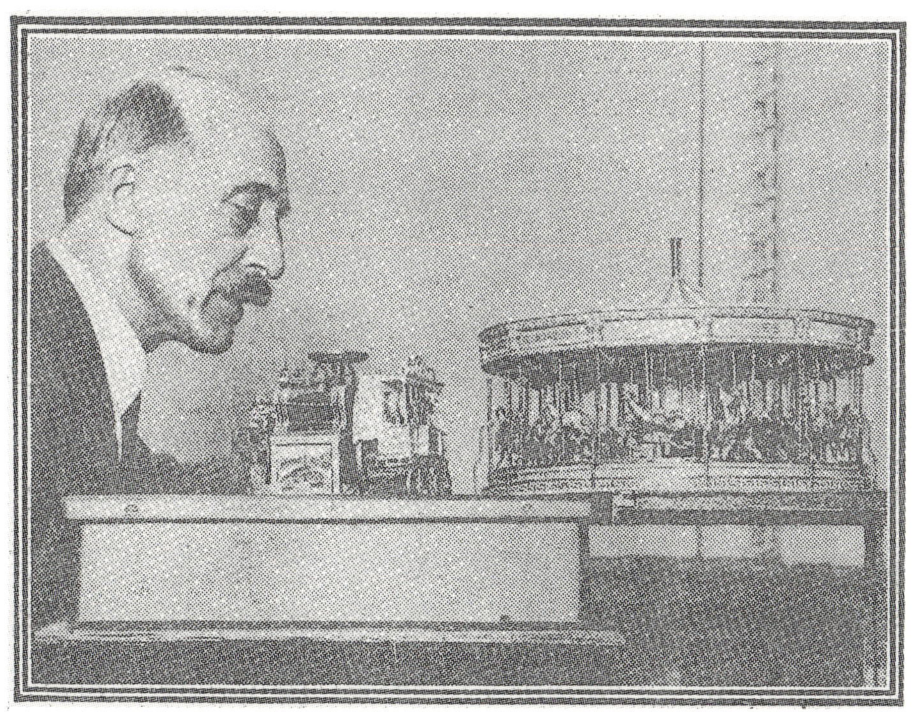

Mr Percy J.Todd with his model roundabout.

To the right: The 1870 map illustrates the land bought by Captain C.R.Knight and his brother-in-law Major R.Spring in 1860 and the roads they had made by 1870. Boundaries of their joint estates were the Blackwater River, London Road, Gibbet Lane and Portsmouth Road.

Below: The portion of the Frimley Park Estate that Captain Knight retained for himself comprised what had previously been Frimley Heath and stretched from Gibbet Lane on the east to a line drawn from Park Street to the Watchetts House and then westwards from there to include the Manor House and its surrounding Park and across the Frimley Road, the Park Farm. Major Spring had the area that was mostly farmland, Watchetts Farm, Hacklane Farm, Bristow Farm, and near the London Road, New Farm. Park Road was cut through their joint estates, and the other roads made through Captain Knight's estate divided off the Tekells Estate from the rest of his property.

London Road is at the top of this picture and Portsmouth Road at the bottom. 1860.

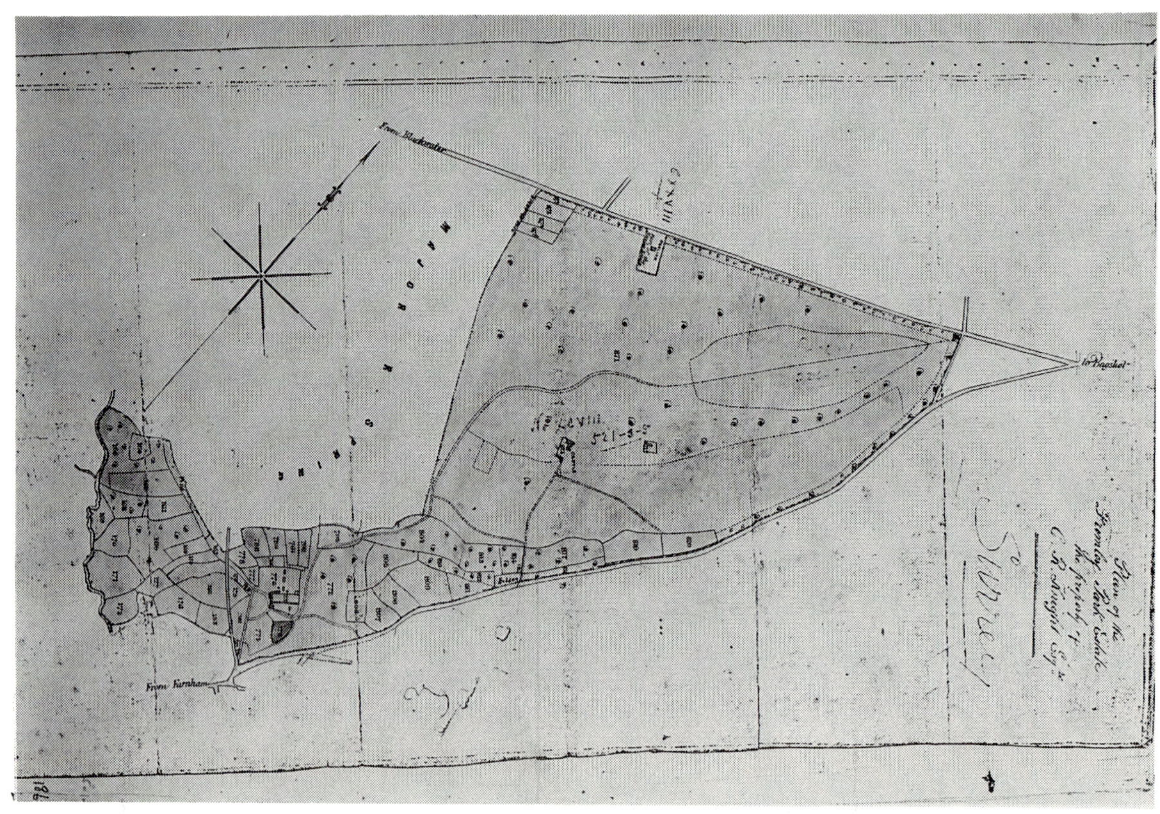

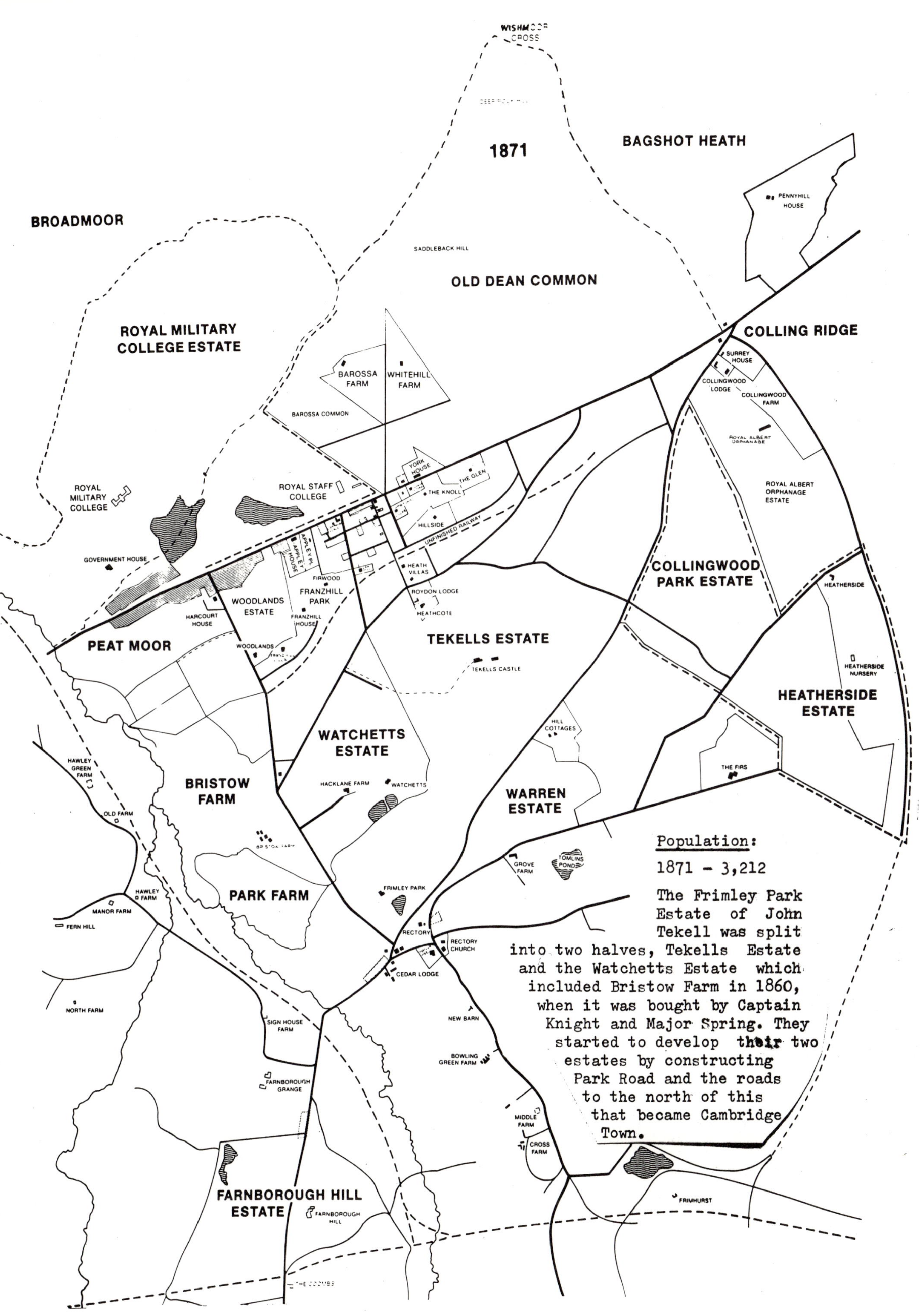

Population:

1871 - 3,212

The Frimley Park Estate of John Tekell was split into two halves, Tekells Estate and the Watchetts Estate which included Bristow Farm in 1860, when it was bought by Captain Knight and Major Spring. They started to develop their two estates by constructing Park Road and the roads to the north of this that became Cambridge Town.

1870. This picture, taken from Crawley Hill looking towards Obelisk Hill, is of the open heathland upon which a part of Camberley has been built. The unfinished railway track is shown running from right to left across the picture and to the rear, near to the London Road, three houses are being erected, probably "Fosse Bank", "The Glen" and "Clarewood". Just to the left of Obelisk Hill a small path can be seen which was to become Knoll Road. The new buildings in Cambridge Town are hidden behind Obelisk Hill, but at its base, to the left, the roof of "Hillside"is just visible.

Left: "Fosse Bank", a house that still exists beside the London Road close to Diamond Hill. The roof of "Portesbery Hill", built at a later date, can be seen to the left. To the right, the Obelisk is plainly visible as a building of four storeys, the top one of which was then above the tree tops. In 1882 it was partly demolished after a fire that it was believed had been started by a band of gypsies.

CHAPTER 7

Captain Knight's development strategy was next concentrated on the area to the east of High Street. He started by constructing a road parallel to High Street, Knoll Road, with two connecting roads, St.George's Road and Portesbery Road. The latter he continued on parallel to the unfinished railway track through fields in which a small stream (The Cam) ran, finally joining it up with Knightsbridge Road. This now gave him the opportunity to sell off this area in building plots of 3-5 acres suitable for the erection of large Victorian houses. Some of these plots stretched right through from the London to the Portesbery Roads.

The first houses built in the London Road were not very far from the Cambridge Hotel. "York House" on the northern side of the road; and almost opposite, where Valroy Close now exists, two more houses, "The Villa" and "Tudor Lodge".

By 1874, two houses in Knoll Road had been built, one being of particular interest, because on this site the Borough of Surrey Heath's new offices now stand. Originally called "Heathfield House", occupied by Miss Eaton, it then became "Cambridge Villa" and later, "Woodbourne", in which there was a very fine dentist's practice from the early 20's to 1984, until the site was purchased by the Borough of Surrey Heath.

Nearby was "The Knoll", a large house with extensive grounds which extended down to Knoll Road. The Camberley Library has now been built there, just in front of where there was once a small pond. In 1875 the Rev. G.B.Cox was the owner of "Knoll House" (now St.Tarcisius School), and he also owned the very wet fields that lay between Knoll Road and the eastern side of the High Street, which he used for grazing cattle.

Just behind "Knoll House", on a steep little hill, was the Obelisk. Its ruin still exists, and there is a path leading to it from the London Road. Built by John Norris, the Squire of Hawley Park House, around 1750, it was then on open moorland. The story goes that he built it to communicate with his friends, the Dashwoods, (of Hell-Fire Club fame) at High Wycombe. By heliograph presumably!

On the southern side of Obelisk Hill, fronting on to Portesbery Road, "Hillside" was built, and this house had a large flat field running alongside Knoll Road which later became a cricket ground. Our Civic Hall and the large open car park by its side now occupy this field, whilst our police station and the school behind are on the hilly part of the "Hillside" estate.

About 1885, with the commencement of housing development in Cambridge Town, the half dozen small semi-detached houses that had been built on the western side of the High Street some ten years previously were converted into shops, and some enlarged. Amongst the occupants of these were Jane Moth, the lady who became the town's first domestic servants agent, and Walter Drake, who started the first livery stables and corn merchants in Camberley.

The western half of the brothers-in-law's estate, Watchetts Lands and Bristow Farm, was almost unaltered except for New Farm, lying just to the east of France Hill which now became Franzhill Park. Quite why this was originally called "Franz", the German for "France", on all the old maps one does not know. A large house was built there about 1870 (now the Adult Education Centre) and the grounds planted with some fine trees to transform the farmland into a lovely park, which became the home of Viscount Southwell. The grounds stretched down to the railway, and not far from this another house was built, "Franzhill Villa", later called "The Whin", in which Major Spring lived, after he sold Watchetts House, and now the site of Robins Bow. The eastern half of New Farm still remained farm land, its farmhouse being re-named "Firwood House".

At the Frimley Road entrance to Franzhill Park was a smithy's forge. Most of the large houses kept many horses in their stables. (Tekells Castle had stabling for 12 horses), and of course all transport was by horse and cart, so there was plenty of work for a blacksmith. Nearby was an Inn very appropriately named "The Four Horseshoes".

France Hill itself was a heavily planted wooded hill, and must have made a fine looking background to Franzhill Park. On the other side of the hill, that nearest to Frimley Road, some small houses were built, and opposite to St.Michaels a few houses had been turned into shops.

St.Michaels Church, with the Vicarage alongside, had been built on Osnaburgh Hill in 1851. At that time the London Road was at a higher level outside the church than it is now, and almost at the same height as the upper portion opposite by the Cinema. But in the 1930's the hump in the road was thought to be dangerous, and a cutting through the hill made to obviate this.

The church stands on a portion of the R.M.C. grounds which had been donated to it by the Treasury. I well remember going to a service there when I was a boy when the famous Army Chaplain of World War I, "Woodbine Willy", the Rev. Geoffrey Kennedy, came to preach there, and packed the church to absolute capacity. He earned his nickname in the war (after a pre-war character in a comic paper) from his gifts of cigarettes to the soldiers in the trenches. We had to arrive at the church more than an hour before the service began, to get in, such was his fame.

In 1868 came the first change in ownership of the brothers-in-law's joint estate. Major Spring sold Bristow Farm and part of the Watchetts Estate to John Hollings, of Wheatley Hall, Bradford.

The part that Hollings bought lay to the south of Park Road, whilst the part to the north was retained by Captain Knight for further development. The fields of Hacklane Farm did not quite reach Park Road in 1868 and so John Hollings purchased the intervening land and also a little land to the east so that the new Watchetts Estate boundaries became Park Road, the Watchetts Stream in the south, Frimley Road to the west and the eastern border was just to the west of where Heatherdale Road and Pine Avenue were constructed some 30 years later. Bristow Farm stretched from the Watchetts Stream in the south to the Peat Moor in the north, and had 133 acres of farmland, whilst the Watchetts Estate now had 188 acres, about half of which was farmland and the other half heath, with two small lakes in the grounds.

A year later, Captain Knight decided to leave Camberley and to reside in Bath, instead of Tekells Castle where he had been living during the past six years. This did not mean that he was abandoning his development plans for Cambridge Town on land to the north of Park Road, only that he decided to sell the Castle and some 330 acres of the surrounding land that lay between

Captain Charles Raleigh Knight: the Founder of Cambridge Town in 1860.

Tekells Castle: The house built by Captain Knight and which he first occupied in 1863. It was situated in a fine Park with beautiful gardens surrounding the house.

Park Road and the Portsmouth Road, bounded on the east by the Church Hill/Crawley Hill Road and on the west by its new border with the Watchetts estate of Mr Hollings, in all about 1/3rd of the total estate that he owned in 1869. (Map, Page 36)

He put this up for sale by private treaty about 1870, and I will give the estate agent's description in full as I think it gives such a wonderful insight into the scale and graciousness of the surroundings in which very wealthy families lived in the Victorian era. This is it:-

Surrey

A desirable Freehold Residential Estate on the High roads from Bagshot to Frimley, close to York and Cambridge Towns, and near to the Royal Military College: comprising 333 acres with an excellent Family Mansion built within the last few years and distinguished as "Tekells Castle".

The district is proverbial for its Healthy Climate and Residential Enjoyments. The soil is a sandy loam on gravel. A great portion of the land is heather clad, and affords most excellent opportunities for sporting.

Tekells Castle comprises an excellent family mansion, on a moderate scale, of imposing elevation, well placed in the middle of a

PARK

Studded with Ornamental Trees and shrubs of fine growth, including some magnificent specimens of "Deodora" "Wellingtonia" "Weymouth Pine" and other choice shrubs of the same class, and surrounded with Fine Belts of firs intersected by
Rides, Drives and Walks, of a most enjoyable character. It is approached by a Carriage Drive, with an ornamental stone-built Entrance Lodge, leading through a plantation intersected by a Stream with a Rustic Bridge over, and winding through the Park.

The Residence

is a substantial structure, with Portico Entrance leading to a fine Entrance Hall having an Oak Floor and Carved Stone Fireplace, Staircase and Gallery, and contains on the upper floor 12 Bed and Dressing Rooms, including Day and Night nurseries. The reception rooms are handsomely fitted with marble chimney pieces and Plate Glass Casement opening to the Gardens and Grounds: they comprise - Handsome Dining Room, elegant Drawing Room, Library, School Room and Conservatory.

The Offices

comprise, spacious Kitchen, Scullery, Store Room, Larder, Pantry, Housekeepers Room, Servants Hall and other requisite offices with excellent cellarage.

The Stabling

is well removed from the Residence and comprises,
Capital Stabling for 12 horses with spacious Coach-houses,
Coachman's House and Harness rooms.

The Gardens and Pleasure Grounds

are laid out with great taste, and dispersed in Grass Terraces, Lawns and Walks: they are handsomely dressed with choice shrubs, Ferns and Flowering Plants in great variety, and there is an excellent Walled Kitchen Garden.

The Park

Is well undulated, and studded with Ornamental Plantations and Trees, and portions are in heather and gorse.

A Second Entrance Lodge

Newly built in brick gives an approach from the Cambridge Town side of the property. There is an excellent homestead (i.e. farmhouse with out-buildings) with all necessary buildings. There is also a
Newly built Cottage Residence known as "Oak Cottage" with garden, admirably situated as a Bailiff's or Steward's residence, and in addition there are two newly built brick cottages occupied by tenants, at rentals amounting to £15 per annum, and also another newly built cottage and garden at present unoccupied.

The entire area proposed to be sold with Tekells Castle comprises

333 Acres

But additional land adjoining can be purchased if desired or the acreage might be reduced.

Tekells Castle and the gardens and Pleasure Grounds surrounding are in the occupation of Mrs Fitzpatrick, and possession will be given of this property at the expiration of her tenancy on Sept. 29, 1875.

....

Captain Knight's wife came from Normandy, and during his occupancy of the Castle he used to travel abroad quite frequently, probably to visit her relatives in France. Whilst he was away his Resident Manager, Mr G Hills, who normally lived at "Oak Cottage" (now One Oak Inn) on the Portsmouth Road border of Tekells Estate, used to move in to look after it. That Captain Knight and his family were good employers, who cared for those who worked for them, and felt a real sense of responsibility for their welfare, is amply described in Daisy Hill's book "Old Frimley". She describes Tekells Castle as "a lovely place with the grounds beautifully laid out. Peacocks spread their fine feathers on the terraces, and the air was full of bird song and the scent of flowers. All the surrounding rough ground running down to what is now Brackendale Road seemed to enhance the beauty of the Park".

Below: The 333 acre Tekells Castle Estate offered for sale by Captain Knight in 1869. Comparison with the 1895 map opposite shows that this estate was at a later date split into four parts, Brackendale Estate, Tekells Castle Estate, Pine Wood Estate and Waverley Estate.

To the top left of this picture, the drive to Tekells Castle later became Heatherdale Road in the Brackendale Estate, whilst just to the right on land retained by Captain Knight, Kingsclear was built.

Brackendale Road and Tekells Avenue were eventually cut through the centre of this portion.

To the top right of the Tekells Castle Estate on land owned by Captain Knight, Branksome Park Road was made later and on the area below this, the Frimley Hall Estate.

Park Road is at the top of the picture and Portsmouth Road at the bottom.

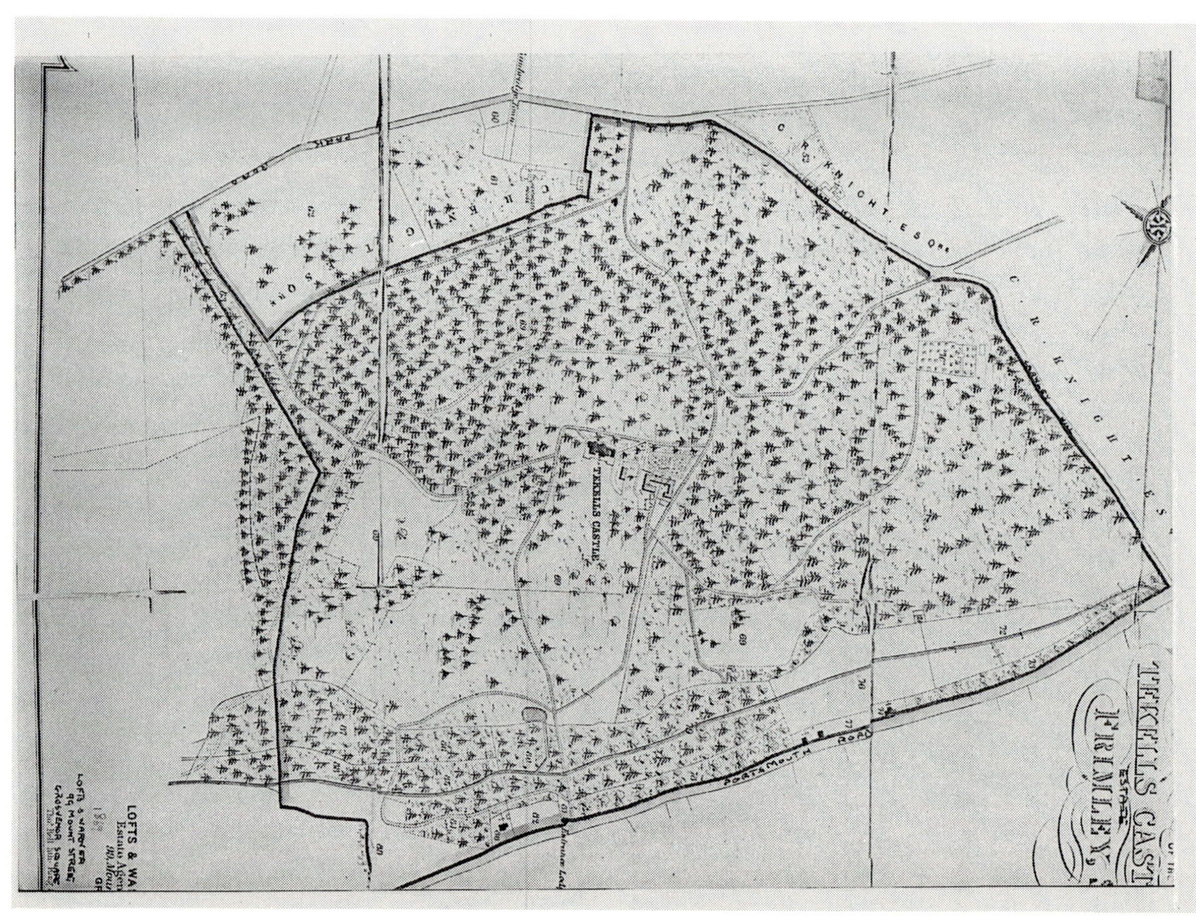

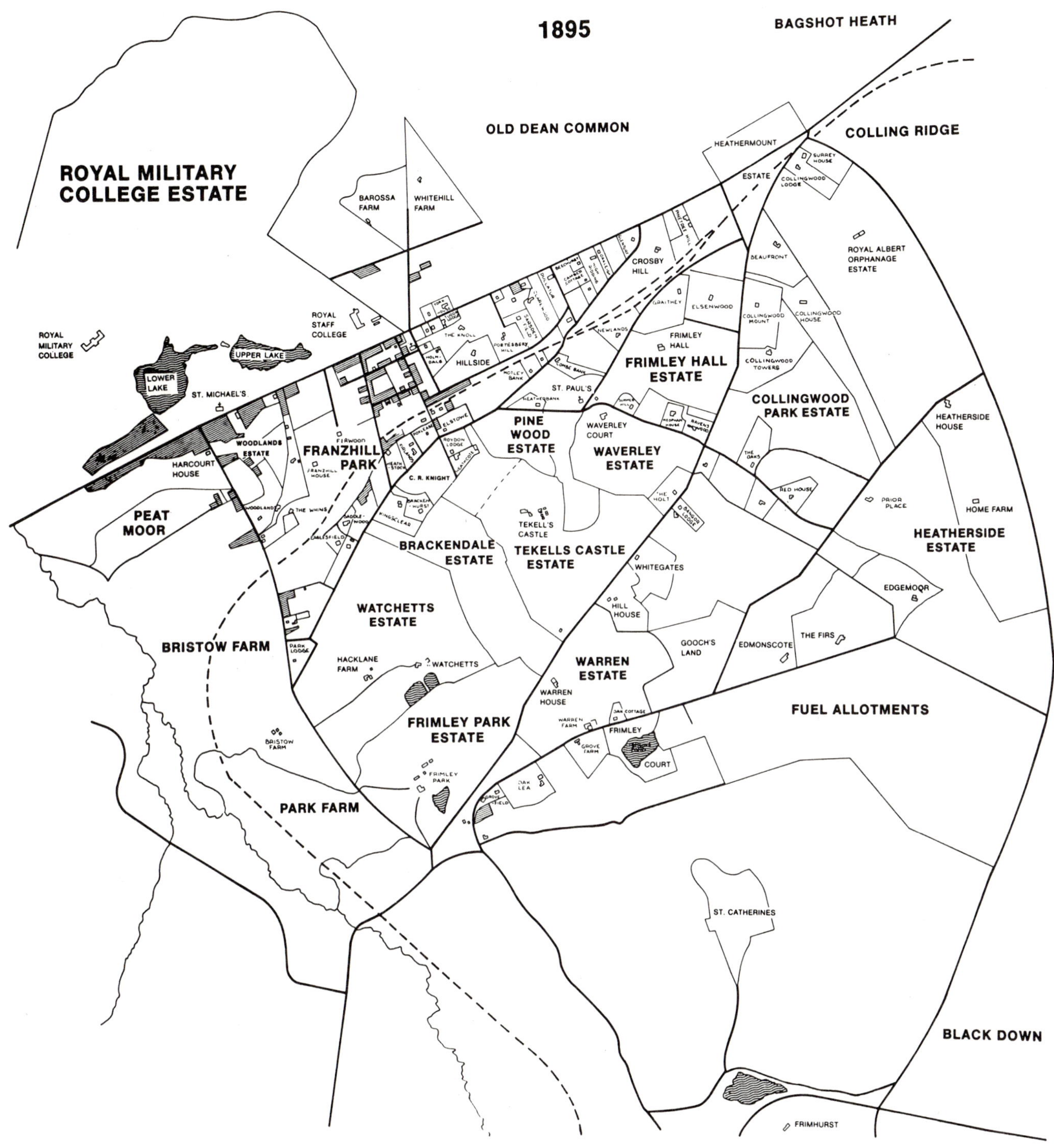

<u>Population:</u>

1891 - 5,295

Tekells Castle Estate had been divided into four parts but had not as yet been further developed. Some large houses set in grounds of from 3 to 30 acres had been built along the London Road on the Frimley Hall and Collingwood Park Estates. The Avenue had been cut through the Woodlands Estate's fir plantation and building also commenced there. The shopping area of Cambridge Town, renamed Camberley in 1877, had developed around the High Street, but Yorktown remained much as it had been 20 years previously.

CHAPTER 8

One of the tenants to whom Captain Knight had let Tekells Castle whilst he was abroad was General Byrne. Now that the 333 acre Tekells estate was on offer, he took the opportunity to buy it despite the fact that he would have to wait until 1875 to take possession of the Castle itself upon the expiration of Mrs Fitzpatrick's lease. Meanwhile, during the next 15 years Captain Knight proceeded to dispose of some of the land still in his possession, and further develop the remainder.

In addition to the land to the north of Park Road, Knight retained one small piece of about 25 acres to the south of the road stretching between Heatherdale Road and Heathway. This was the land on which he had built "Heathcote" and "Roydon Lodge" and on which "Kingsclear" and "Brackenhurst" were to be built at a later date.

He also retained the area he owned to the north of the Church Hill/Crawley Hill roads through which Crawley Ridge Road and the railway run. In 1879 he sold one half of this, the 114 acre estate that lay between the Portsmouth Road and Crawley Ridge Road, to Mr Thomas Boys (of whom more in the next chapter), retaining a part interest himself. In turn, Mr Boys sold about half of this to Mr G.W.Fowler in 1881, who built Frimley Hall there with its surrounding parkland. Two other estates of about 12-15 acres were also sold nearby, in which "Graitney" and "High Beeches" (afterwards named "Elsenwood") were built, and to the north of these a triangular estate was purchased by Mr William Powell, an architect, who then re-sold it to Mr J.Lydall who built "Lauriston" there.

Graitney House, now demolished to make way for Crawley Middle School, was built about 1890 for Captain (later Vice-Admiral) Johnstone, and Elsenwood was built at the same time by the Van der Byl family, who owned this estate right up to the time that it was sold for housing development in 1953.

During Vice-Admiral Johnstone's lifetime, in 1896, he rented Graitney to the Crown Prince of Siam who was to undergo a training course at Sandhurst. The Prince was there until 1898, when he left Graitney and moved to Frimley Park Manor House which he then rented for a short time.

In 1982, long after the Crown Prince had left England, a deputation from Siam arrived at Crawley Middle School and asked to see the place where their Prince had lived for a time in Camberley. They were members of a committee set up by the present King of Thailand to celebrate the centenary of King Vajirauudh's birth (our Crown Prince's father) and to research into his life. The party were headed on their visit by our Minister of Education.

Vice-Admiral Johnstone sold Graitney in 1920 to Mr J.E.Cubitt, who had just returned from India where he had worked for 20 years in a jute company in Calcutta. His son later became a well-known architect and sculptor, for which he received the MBE.

The house was of the large Victorian variety, with 8 bedrooms for the family and their guests, a servants' hall, butler's pantry and five bedrooms for servants "living in". The Stabling had 2 stalls and a loose box, harness room, 2 double Coach Houses with grooms' bedrooms above.

Graitney, now demolished to make way for Crawley Middle School, was once the home of Vice Admiral Johnstone, who rented it for two years to the Crown Prince of Siam when he was at Sandhurst.

Elsenwood, the home of the Van Der Byl family. No longer in existence, but once situated near to Frimley Hall, as was Graitney.

It had a beautiful garden, where Captain Johnstone had planted some exotic trees and shrubs which he had collected from all over the world. Wellingtonias, cedars, cypresses, magnolias, azaleas, camellias were there, and a specimen tulip tree is still in the grounds of the school.

Vice-Admiral Johnstone achieved a certain kind of fame when he was the Flag Captain to Rear Admiral Markham, wearing his flag in HMS Camperdown, and was taking part in manoeuvres off Tripoli in 1893 with another squadron commanded by Vice-Admiral Sir George Tryon, wearing his flag in HMS Victoria. Owing to a tragic mistake by Vice-Admiral Tryon, there was a collision and the Victoria was sunk with much loss of life. There was a court martial afterwards at which the surviving officers were exonerated from blame, but later, there was much controversy over the manoeuvres which had caused the accident, and whether or not they should have been ordered.

Strange to say, two other naval officers who lived in this district were present at this naval disaster. One was the midshipman son of Captain Gambier RN, who lived at "Mylncroft" Frimley, who tragically lost his life while serving in HMS Victoria, and the other was a young lieutenant (who afterwards became the famous Admiral Sturdee) who was serving in the Camperdown, but survived.

In 1873, work on the railway track recommenced, and this cut the area retained by Captain Knight that lay between Park Road/Middleton Road and Crawley Ridges Road into two pieces. South of the railway St Pauls Church Hall was built in 1895 on Crawley Hill and was used as a church until 1902. The present church was completed in 1907, when services commenced there, and is Scandinavian in its design. "Heatherbank" is the oldest house in this area and still exists on the left hand side of Church Hill. "Newlands" and "Combe Bank" were both there in 1895, but "Old Dean Hall", built by Mr G.Fowler, is of later date.

Now that the railway's completion was certain, it was sure to bring more people to live in Camberley, and so Captain Knight decided to start the construction of another road, situated in close proximity to the railway track, but just to the south of it. This was Gordon Road. By 1880 it had been made from its junction with West Street, westwards as far as Gordon Crescent which connected it with Park Road, and there it remained for many years, until finally Gordon Avenue was added on to join it up with the Frimley Road. Park Road and Gordon Road were additionally linked together by Garfield Road and Firlands Road as well as by Park Street and Heathcote Road. Each of these areas so divided was now sold for building and one, or at the most two, houses built on each plot which was of 2-3 acres. The land between Gordon Road and the railway was divided into plots of about ½ acre or less, and sold for much smaller houses to be built there. In fact, these were almost the first "middle class" houses in Camberley.

Captain Knight did not build in this area himself, instead he sold the land lying between Park Road and Gordon Road to Mr Boys for development in 1884, and later Mr William Watson acquired the land between Gordon Road and the railway.

"Heath Villas", which Knight had built earlier, now became "Heathdene". "Elstowe" was built where the Abbey Court block of flats are now, and on the other side of Heathcote Road, "Foxlease", which became the home of Dr Cadell, and later Elmhurst School. In the next plot to "Foxlease" on the west side of Firlands Road was "Firlands House", which became Camberley Court Hotel in the 1950's, but is now demolished and replaced by the

Camberley Court Gardens block of flats. On the estate between Garfield Road and Gordon Crescent two houses were built, "Saddlewood" and "Broomfield", in which I have an especial interest. This was once the home of Colonel Chenevix-Trench, but my father bought it when it was offered for sale in 1960 as a speculation. He never lived there, but let it to Mrs Winterbourne for her to start St Catherine's School, which it still is today. The property now belongs to Kingsclear Old Folks home to whom it was bequeathed after my father's death.

"Eaglesfield" on the western side of Gordon Crescent and "Saddlewood" (now become a housing development) were both built on the site of dwellings that were there in 1823, alongside the ancient track that led from the Watchetts to New Farm.

The Woodlands Estate, lying between the France Hill Estate (New Farm) and Frimley Road, did not belong to Major Spring or Captain Knight. This land, together with a smaller piece on the western side of Frimley Road, had been awarded to Joseph Graves under the 1801 Frimley Enclosure Act.

Development commenced there about 1870 when a road was made through the wooded plantation on France Hill. This was at first called "Plantation Road", but was later re-named "The Avenue". To the west of this Heatherley Road was joined, and from the Frimley Road, Woodlands Road ran round a field which had been called "Roundabout" on the 1842 Tithe Map. Land was sold bordering these roads and moderately sized houses started to appear. These were very conveniently situated between the Staff College and the R.M.C. and quite a few of them were built with the intention of letting them to married officers on the Staff College courses, for at that time no "Army owned" properties were available for this purpose. In fact this was the situation right up until 1950, when the first married officers quarters were built by the Army near Barossa.

On the Yorktown side of Frimley Road, Vale Road was started and ten small houses built there. On Mr Graves' land to the east of the Duke of York Hotel along the London Road, a number of small houses were built and one larger one, "Osnaburgh House", which was bought by Colonel B.M.Dawes.

The last surviving building of the Royal Albert Orphanage, the chapel, was destroyed by fire in 1987. This is it.

CHAPTER 9

When Captain Knight bought John Tekell's Frimley Park Estate in 1860, his purchase comprised all the land to the north and west of the Portsmouth Road, but the triangular area to the south and east of this bounded by Portsmouth Road, the Maultway and the lower Chobham Road/Bisley Road was not part of Knight's Estate. This area was divided into two sections by the Upper Chobham Road, and practically all of this land had been allocated, by the 1801 Enclosure Act, to just four men, with James Laurell getting the lion's share. (Map, Page 7)

Three-quarters of the northernmost section, called "Cart Bottom", had been planted with pines by Laurell in 1802 and, by 1865, these had become sizeable trees ready for commercial tree-felling. Because of its proximity to Colling Ridge, this plantation was known as Colling Wood. The other half of Cart Bottom, stretching towards Frimley, was heathland with a number of steep little hills and clumps of pine trees which, some 50 years later, was to become Camberley Heath Golf Course, and this was owned by Thomas Knight. Still nearer to Frimley were some fields which were a part of the original Manor Estate, and these later became Warren Farm.

The southernmost section lying to the south-east of Upper Chobham Road was "Stake Bottom", now known as Heatherside. It was one of the highest parts of Camberley, open moorland and only wooded on its lower slopes.

In 1862 two hundred acres of Cart Bottom adjacent to the Maultway, once partly owned by Timothy Curtis and partly by James Laurell, were sold to the Royal Albert Orphanage Trust. This was a public subscription Trust that had been formed to purchase a site and thereon erect an orphanage as a memorial to Prince Albert, who had died in 1861. The Orphanage was completed in 1864, but sadly the last surviving building, the chapel, was destroyed by fire in 1987. Admission to the Orphanage had to be sponsored by subscribers to the Trust, and both boys and girls were admitted. They were not only educated there, but were also taught trades that might be useful to them to enable them to earn their living as adults. Collingwood Farm was a part of the Estate, its farmhouse being situated by the Chobham Road, and was used to train the children in husbandry as well as to provide them with food. At the end of World War II, the Orphanage was amalgamated with the Royal Alexandria School and moved to Gatton Park near Reigate. The buildings were sold to the M.O.D. for the W.R.A.C. officer-cadet training centre. Since then, with their removal to the R.M.A.Sandhurst, the estate has become vacant and at the present time there is a proposal to site a 400 house estate there.

Most of the land enclosed by James Laurell in 1801, with the exception of that sold to Tekell, remained in his possession until after he had left Frimley in 1837 and until his death, which I presume would have been in about 1860 since he was a contemporary of Tekell. I believe that he too had no children and, therefore, it would have been his widow who proceeded to sell off his remaining Frimley Manor lands.

In 1872, Messes. Daniel, Smith and Oakley were instructed to put up for sale the southern half of the original Frimley Manor, i.e. the farmlands to the south of Chobham/Bisley Roads. This they did after first dividing it into 16 lots. About the same time Mr William Kingdom purchased Colling Wood, which was not included in this sale, but sold separately.

Mr Thomas Boys, whom we have met in our last chapter, now came on to the scene. He was a Wine Merchant with premises in Regent Street, London, and a home in Tunbridge Wells. He was also a very considerable land and property speculator, owning shops and houses in the Shepherds Bush, Fulham and Putney areas, and also land in Ashstead, Surrey. Perhaps he saw the Tekell's Estate sale notice in "The Times" in 1859, but found that the land had already been bought prior to the auction. Upon looking around he later discovered that Colling Wood might be put on the market and, when the opportunity came, purchased the land.

Whatever the circumstances were, we find that, by 1871, a house called "Collingwood Park" had been built in the area, previously owned by Mr Kingdom, that lay between the Royal Albert Orphanage Estate and the Portsmouth Road in Cart Bottom. This was now the Collingwood Park Estate, with Mr Thomas Boys named as the owner of the house which, at a later date, was re-named "Collingwood Mount". Originally called Laurell's Fir Plantation, the estate was heavily wooded and had a number of paths through its coppice that stemmed from an avenue of pines planted along a road that had been made in the southern part of the estate known as "Collingwood Road", (re-named "Prior Road" some 35 years later).

Mr Boys had a friend, Mr Flaxman, with whom he had had some property deals in London, and the two became involved in the development of the Collingwood Park Estate. Whether or not he was a relative as well as a friend of Mr Boys, I do not know but, in 1915 when Mr Boys died, a very wealthy man, he appointed Mr Flaxman to be one of the two trustees charged with the task of administering his estate.

The Collingwood Park Estate was one of about 185 acres, and large building plots were offered for sale with a title that commenced on April 11th, 1867, which presumably was the date on which Thomas Boys acquired the land from Mr Kingdom. The first plots sold were in the northern part of the estate, all four of which were of about 25 acres and carried a covenant by which no dwelling-house costing less that £1,000 could be erected on the plot. Remembering that this was a very large sum in those days, one can see that Mr Boys intended this area to be very "up-market". He pursued the same policy throughout the disposal of the rest of the estate when Springfield Road was built as a loop from Collingwood Road and plots sold alongside these two roads about 1885-1900.

Between 1871 and 1895, "Maywood", "Collingwood House" and "Collingwood Tower" were built on 25 acre estates surrounding "Collingwood Park". Strange to say, all four of these houses were re-named before long, becoming "Beaufront", "Hillcrest", "Mulroy House" and "Collingwood Mount" respectively. In 1901 another estate was sold just to the south of these to Major General England, who built "Cleughbrae" there.

Along the Collingwood Road, "Lhasa" and "Highland View" were built on its southern side, and "The Oaks" and "Red House" on its northern. The first three were later re-named "Southcote Lodge", "Prior Croft" and "Dundaff Muir", but "Red House" retained its name until it was demolished about 1965.

All these houses have had an interesting history. "Maywood" (Beaufront) belonged to Mr Flaxman in 1887, but he soon let it to two sisters, the Misses Carr, who opened a boarding school for young ladies, called Mayfield School. They were there until 1913 when their headmistress, Miss Rimington, took over from them. In 1920 she bought the property from Mr Flaxman and

Collingwood Towers (Mulroy House), first owned by Richard Ansdell the Victorian artist famous for his pictures of sporting occasions. In the 1920's it became the home of the Spanish Ambassador, the Marquis de Villespar. The house no longer exists, but the estate of the house which runs alongside the M3 has been named Iberian Way to commemorate its Spanish connection.

Collingwood Park House (Collingwood Mount), was the first house built on the Collingwood Park Estate. The owners can be seen sitting on the verandah just above the steps to the right, looking out on to their beautifully kept gardens.

re-named it "Beaufront" and also similarly, the school. It remained there until the start of World War II, and "Beaufront's" further history is recounted in Chapter 28.

"Collingwood House" (Hillcrest) was owned by Colonel Cubitt in 1896, and about 1907 by Mr W.E.Johnson, an Ironmaster industrialist from Birmingham. His niece, Miss Johnson, who lived there later, came from Australia and spent much of her time transcribing books for the blind into Braille. The house was actually on the Colling Ridge in one of the most commanding sites in the whole of Collingwood Park. Chatsworth Heights and Hillcrest Road occupy this estate now. "Hillcrest" has also been called "Collingwood Hall".

The land upon which the house was built originally belonged to Mr Flaxman, and extended right down to Upper Chobham Road, but when he sold it to Colonel Cubitt, he divided off the southernmost part of this estate and retained it himself until 1912, when he sold it to form part of Camberley Heath Golf Course.

"Collingwood Park" (Collingwood Mount), the first house on the whole estate, must have been built about 1868. In 1896 it was owned by General Lempriere and his family until 1936, when Colonel Foley and Lady Berkeley resided there. It has now been demolished and another large house, which is in flats, built on the site, also called "Collingwood Mount". The grounds of its estate are occupied by Collingwood Rise and Loddon Close.

"Collingwood Towers" (Mulroy House) was built about 1873, and its first owner was Richard Ansdell R.A. a Victorian artist. After his death it was let for a short while and then purchased by Colonel T.Harris, who was there until 1922. In 1926 it was sold to the Spanish ambassador, the Marquis of Villespar, who bought it with the intention of providing a possible refugee home for King Alfonso XIII of Spain should his monarchy be deposed. A Dictatorship had been set up in Spain in 1923 with General Primo de Rivera at its head. This eventually caused the King to flee from his country in 1931 and Spain then became a Republic. However, when this eventually happened, Alfonso decided to take up residence in Italy instead of England, and the "Towers" was sold.

In 1935 H.H.the Maharaja Jam Sahib of Nawanger rented the house for a short period. He was a relative of the famous cricketer Ranjit Sinjhi, and was much in demand locally to open fetes etc. The next owner was Mr Vandespar, a gentleman who had seen much service abroad in India. He brought two Indian servants with him from his Far Eastern travels who were very devoted to him and accompanied him everywhere he went. The further history of "Collingwood Towers", which is combined with that of "Beaufront", is told in a later chapter, as is that of "Cleughbrae". Iberian Way now occupies a part of "Mulroy's" estate, so named because of the house's connection with Spain.

"Lhasa" (Southcote Lodge) in Prior Road was, so I am told, at one time occupied by one of the Younghusband family, the explorer of Tibet. I have been unable to find evidence of this, although it may well have been so as another gentleman who was also connected with the exploration of Tibet, Colonel Ryder, lived nearby in 1926. In 1896 the house was owned by Mr Emmanuel Moor and I think it had also been built for him. From 1907 onwards it had a series of tenants, amongst whom was De Laslo R.A. who painted the Queen Mother's portrait whilst he lived here. I believe that Michael Medwin, the actor, was also a tenant at one time. The house was demolished at the time that the M3 was built, and Prior Road diverted at Ravenswood cross roads junction. Prior Heath First School's playing fields now occupy a part of "Lhasa" grounds, which had become known as "Southcote Lodge Farm" by then.

On the same side of the road was "Highland View" (Prior Croft) with a windmill in its grounds. This was owned by Major-General Maurice, a soldier who was also a military historian of renown. Almost opposite was the "Red House", owned by Major-General Brooke Chambers, who later moved to Church Hill and lived at "Brooks Court", a house previously called "Tekells House" (not to be confused with Tekells Castle). After he left, the house was sold to the Van der Velde's, whose friend was Bret Harte, the famous American novelist. He died there in 1902 and was buried in St.Peters churchyard, Frimley.

Left: Collingwood House (Hillcrest) was sited on Colling Ridge and its stable block, pictured below, had a clock tower that was something of a local landmark. The house had two driveways leading to it from the Portsmouth Road, one of these is now Hillcrest Road and the other Chatsworth Heights. A portion of the original estate which stretched to the Upper Chobham Road is now a part of Camberley Heath Golf Course.

CHAPTER 10

Meanwhile, in Stake Bottom a most interesting newcomer arrived in 1860. He was a Swiss botanist named Augustus Mongredien who bought 300 acres of heath land adjoining the Maultway to the south of Upper Chobham Road from James Laurell, with the intention of starting a silk-worm farm there. The area chosen had previously been called New Zealand, but he re-named it "Heatherside".

In order to purchase the land, he obtained a mortgage from Sir Gabriel Goldney. Sir Gabriel came from Chippenham in Wiltshire, and was their Member of Parliament in 1865. He lived there and was listed in "Who was Who" as a landed proprietor, owning 2,800 acres around Corsham, an estate about twice as large as John Tekell's, which embraced about 3/5ths of Camberley. Sir Gabriel had three sons, Prior, Frederick and John, all of whom became barristers attaining renown as Recorder of Helston, High Sherrif of Wiltshire and Chief Justice of Trinidad respectively. The family had become well known in the West Country, both as merchant bankers and also as highly successful traders. It had two branches, one of which had originally been clothiers based in Chippenham, and the other, grocers based in Bristol. The latter branch of the family were Quakers, and Thomas Goldney was one of the merchant venturers who financed shipping voyages from that port. The house in which the family lived at Clifton is now used to accommodate students at Bristol University. The Chippenham branch of the family were granted a Baronetage in 1880 and, both Sir Prior in 1900 and Sir Frederick in 1925, succeeded to Sir Gabriel's title and resided in Camberley, playing a part in the town's development.

Mongredien was a renowned horticulturist, and he spent a fortune on his venture. Heatherside House was built and a manager, Mr Thornton, installed there with a large and extravagant staff. Some 40 or more girls were brought up daily from Bagshot to deal with the products of the silk worms. But the winds over the Chobham Ridges proved to be too cold for silk worms, the venture was scrapped and the estate devoted to growing trees instead. A mile long avenue of Wellintonias was planted to provide a windbreak, and also many other exotic trees and shrubs, and in 1870 he wrote an authoritative text-book on this subject. In 1874 his Nursery was turned into a Company, but Mongredien appears to have lived in London and only visited the Nursery occasionally. Thornton was a poor manager, with the result that the Company soon went bankrupt and Sir Gabriel Goldney foreclosed on the mortgage, taking possession of both the Nursery Garden venture and Heatherside House. He lived there for two years, but afterwards it was let on short leases to numerous tenants until Dr Walter Leaf bought the house and 8 acres in 1906. Dr Leaf was a classical scholar as well as being chairman of the Westminster Bank, and spent a great deal of money on enlarging and reconstructing the house. But he <u>did</u> object to the smells that came from the Piggery Outhouses of Collingwood Farm situated immediately opposite to him on the other side of Upper Chobham Road, and in order to obviate this he purchased the land on which the farm buildings stood from the Royal Albert Orphanage, who then moved the farm up closer to the Orphanage.

After the departure of Mr Thornton, Mr Frederick Street became Sir Gabriel's manager of the Nursery Garden and agent for the house, and was succeeded by his son in 1895. But about 1917 he had a disagreement with Sir Prior Goldney and left to set up on his own in West End.

"Return from the Ride", by Charles Wellington Furse depicts himself and his beautiful wife by the Chobham Ridges where their home, Yockley House, was situated.

DAME KATHERINE FURSE
DIRECTOR W.R.N.S. 1917-1919

Yockley House is one of the most elegant Victorian houses that still exist in Camberley. It is at the southernmost end of the avenue of Wellingtonia trees on the Heatherside Estate.

The Wellingtonias that can be seen for miles around on the Finchampstead Ridges came from the Heatherside Nurseries. Apparently the owner of this land about 1880, had had an awkward "right of way" problem there, and said that if people would forego other paths through his land he would build them a road to use with the avenue of trees, which have now become a landmark for many miles around.

After Mongredien left Heatherside in 1875, Sir Gabriel constructed Goldney Road as a continuation of Collingwood Road into the Heatherside area, and the central area leading from The Nursery was turned into Home Farm which Sir Gabriel rented to tenant farmers. From 1908 - 1920 this farm was leased by the Stokes family, and in those days all the milk that their dairy sold came from there. This is the same family whose large dairy in Pembroke Way is the major milk and dairy produce supplier in Camberley at the present time.

About 1885 "Prior Place" was built as a home for Prior Goldney's family, sited close to the Upper Chobham Road, and this house still exists. Yockley House was also built about this time, and is still there, close to the Maultway at the start of the Wellingtonia avenue of trees. In 1900 Charles Wellington Furse A.R.A., a famous Victorian artist lived here. His best known work, "Diana of the Uplands", has Chobham Ridges as a background. He had an even more famous wife, Dame Katharine Furse, who was largely responsible for the development of the Voluntary Aid Detachments in World War I, and was afterwards the first Director of the W.R.N.S., for which service she was created a D.B.E. in 1917, having been largely instrumental in the foundation of the Womens Royal Naval Service. She had only been married for four years before her husband died in 1904, and was a widow at the time of her war service years. She died in 1952, and both she and her husband are buried in St.Peters churchyard.

To the south of Heatherside Nurseries, and adjacent to the Bisley Road, the Brompton Hospital purchased a 20 acre site from Sir Gabriel for £3,900 in order to build a Sanatorium. In 1900, tuberculosis, or consumption as it was usually called, was the great killer of mankind, just as cancer has become this in more recent times. One third of the entire population died from this one disease. Because of the pines and the high ground, the medical profession were of the opinion that an area such as Camberley was very suitable for tubercular patients, particularly for those who were convalescing, often for long periods, after having received treatment in the London Brompton Hospital, (which had been opened in 1846).

In the "Morning Post" of 1883 there appeared a letter from a physician about the Camberley District, in which he said:

> "As a physician I am asked day after day where is the best quarter to go for quickly recruiting the health, or where is the healthiest spot to reside within a handy distance of town. What I can and do tell them may be a boon to others to know. Nowhere within 100 miles of London is there such dry and bracing air and it is marvellous to witness how rapidly tubercular affection of the chest, asthma, deranged livers and rheumatic gout in all its forms there disappear. I formerly sent many to Scotland or abroad, but happily there is better than either at hand. To the north of the Chobham Ridges and westward of the Duke of Connaughts (Bagshot Park) are several square miles of the wildest and most charming scenery of forest and heath land belonging to various

> parishes, kept open for ever under Her Majesty's Inclosure Commissioners. Heath land is healthier than grass or cultivated land in so far that heather absorbs but little moisture, and there is barely any decay in it".

The London Brompton Hospital which had by 1899 found it increasingly difficult to accommodate patients suffering from tuberculosis, decided that Camberley's Heatherside Estate was the best place available for their Sanatorium. The site was purchased, the Sanatorium built and in 1904 it was opened by the Prince and Princess of Wales. (Map, Page 67)

The patients, many of whom were there for long periods, performed light tasks, such as cleaning and gardening. They even helped to build a reservoir in the grounds, presumably when they were nearly fit again. In the first 6 years of its existence some 1,700 patients were treated, and very few died.

Tuberculosis ceased to be the great killer disease just after World War II when the streptomycin drugs were discovered and, as TB became a comparatively rare disease, so the hospital changed from being a TB Sanatorium, first into a more general hospital and then into what it has now become, a psychiatric hospital.

At about the same time, just to the south of Goldney Road, "Edgemoor" was built, the birthplace of Miss Grace Reynolds, who did so much for young people in the town, and especially for the Frimley and Camberley Cadet Corps. She was awarded the M.B.E. for her services and there is a "Walk" in Camberley Town Centre named after her in memory of her achievements.

Leaving Heatherside, which terminates at "Edgemoor", we arrive at another large estate of approximately 60 acres lying between the Bisley and Upper Chobham Roads on Frimley Ridge, comprising the area that had been enclosed by the Hon. Alexander Murray in 1801. "Eastlea Court" (The Firs) was built here, and about 1875 it also had a Summer House in its grounds. By 1895 this had been enlarged and separated from the Eastlea Court Estate, becoming "Edmonscote", whose grounds are now occupied by Ravenscote School.

The original owner of "Eastlea Court" was a Mr J.Graves, possibly a member of the same family that developed the Woodlands Estate in Yorktown, granted to them under the Enclosure Act. About 1910 the Astleys lived in "Eastlea Court", and the Temple-Cookes in "Edmonscote". The former were an elderly, but wealthy, couple, and they had a beautiful house with fine furniture. They used to drive out in a smart carriage with a coachman and footman on the box.

Mr Temple-Cooke was a barrister who became the Recorder of Southampton, and also the Counsel to the Admiralty on circuit. When his family first came to Edmonscote they owned a horse and carriage but this was quickly superceded by one of the new-fangled motor cars then in their pioneering days! He was a friend of Mr J.F.Wright of Frimley Hall, and between them they were the prime movers in the foundation of Camberley Heath Golf Club, of which more in a later chapter.

Another estate in this area was "The Warren". It comprised some 100 acres situated near to Frimley village, previously a part of the original Frimley Manor. Mr Dunham built "Warren House" there in 1871, but in 1882 he sold it to a family of three sisters, the Misses Connop. Daisy Hill's book, "Old Frimley", gives a delightful description of her family's life "in service" there and on their farm. The last of the three sisters, Miss Emily, died in 1917 and the estate was bequeathed to her nephew Colonel Newland, in whose family it remained until 1956 when it was sold for housing development, the first "private" estate south of the Portsmouth Road, sold for development after World War II.

Brompton Hospital, opened in 1904 as a Sanatorium for patients suffering from tuberculosis, is on the Heatherside Estate.

Long term patients helping with the excavation of the resevoir in the grounds of Brompton Hospital

CHAPTER 11

On the southern side of Bisley Road, stretching from Tomlins Pond over Jackpond Hill towards Deepcut, was a 350 acre area of pine-clad heathland which became a Poors Allotment for the benefit of the inhabitants of Frimley in 1826. This is known today as the Frimley Fuel Allotments. Because it has become the subject of so much controversy in recent times and also because the preservation of this area as an "open breathing space" in our town is of such importance to us all, the author hopes he will be forgiven for recounting its history somewhat fully. (Map, Page 37)

Fuel Allotments came into being when the Enclosure Commissioners were required by law to set aside a portion of common land from their enclosures, in order to provide a reasonable supply of fuel for the poor of a district, who were deemed to be those who did not occupy land or houses that had a yearly value (in 1826) of £5.

As Trustees, to administer the allotments, they appointed the Lord of the Manor, the Rector, Churchwarden and Overseers of the Poor in each district, and charged them with the task of distributing the fuel according to regulations the Trustees themselves decided upon. At first the fuel consisted of tree-tops that had been cut down by the foresters in the course of their duties, but sand and gravel when available were also allowed to be taken. As the years went by, the Trusteeship was altered to include representatives from the Urban District Council, and instead of fuel being taken from the Allotment the poor of the district were given money in lieu.

The Charity Commissioners had the ownership of the land invested in themselves, but had the right to authorise the Trustees to sell portions of the land from time to time, and with the money so obtained, to invest it to produce money for fuel and warm blankets for the poor.

In 1903 the Commissioners varied the regulations they gave to the Trustees to allow them to let a portion of the land for agricultural allotments, and later this was again varied to enable them to let land on the Allotment for a period of 22 years maximum, providing that public notice of their intention to do so had previously been given in an adequate manner. One of the provisions named being that part of the rent so obtained was to be applied to making recreation grounds or field gardens available to the people of Frimley. Another provision required that the Trustees should allow no part of the Allotment to be enclosed or built upon, and also reasonable access to the land should be allowed to the public.

The original 350 acres of the Allotment were reduced by 76 acres sold to Eliza Pain in 1861 (St. Catherines Estate) for £1,012, and 10.4 acres sold for £68,000 in 1960 to provide Tomlinscote School with its playing fields.

In 1986, a proposal was made by the Trustees to let about half of the land then existing for a public golf course to be constructed thereon. A long lease was proposed that would have ensured that this land was preserved as an open breathing space for the inhabitants of Frimley for the next 125 years, as well as providing an appreciable income for Charitable purposes.

That this scheme offered considerable attractions not only for its recreational value, but also, judging by Camberley's experience whereby their golf course had become almost the only "breathing space" oasis left in a desert of solid residential development, makes it hard to understand the vociferous objections to it raised by a section of the Frimley inhabitants. Especially as the alternative they proposed, that of starting to sell a part of the land to builders, and trying to get an assurance from the Charity Commissioners that if they did agree to this, they would then covenant to sell off no other part of the Allotment in the future, was not given to them.

One can only hope that our local Borough councillors will be strong enough to withstand the building developers' attempts to get a foothold on this land, almost the last large estate of moorland left to us, and so preserve it for us all by denying building planning permission on any part of the Fuel Allotments, for it would seem that we can expect little help from the Charity's Commissioners in this respect. Surely a public golf course which thousands of people could enjoy on half the site, whilst the other half was preserved as a moorland walking space without any housing development, was the ideal way of preserving this amenity for the town!

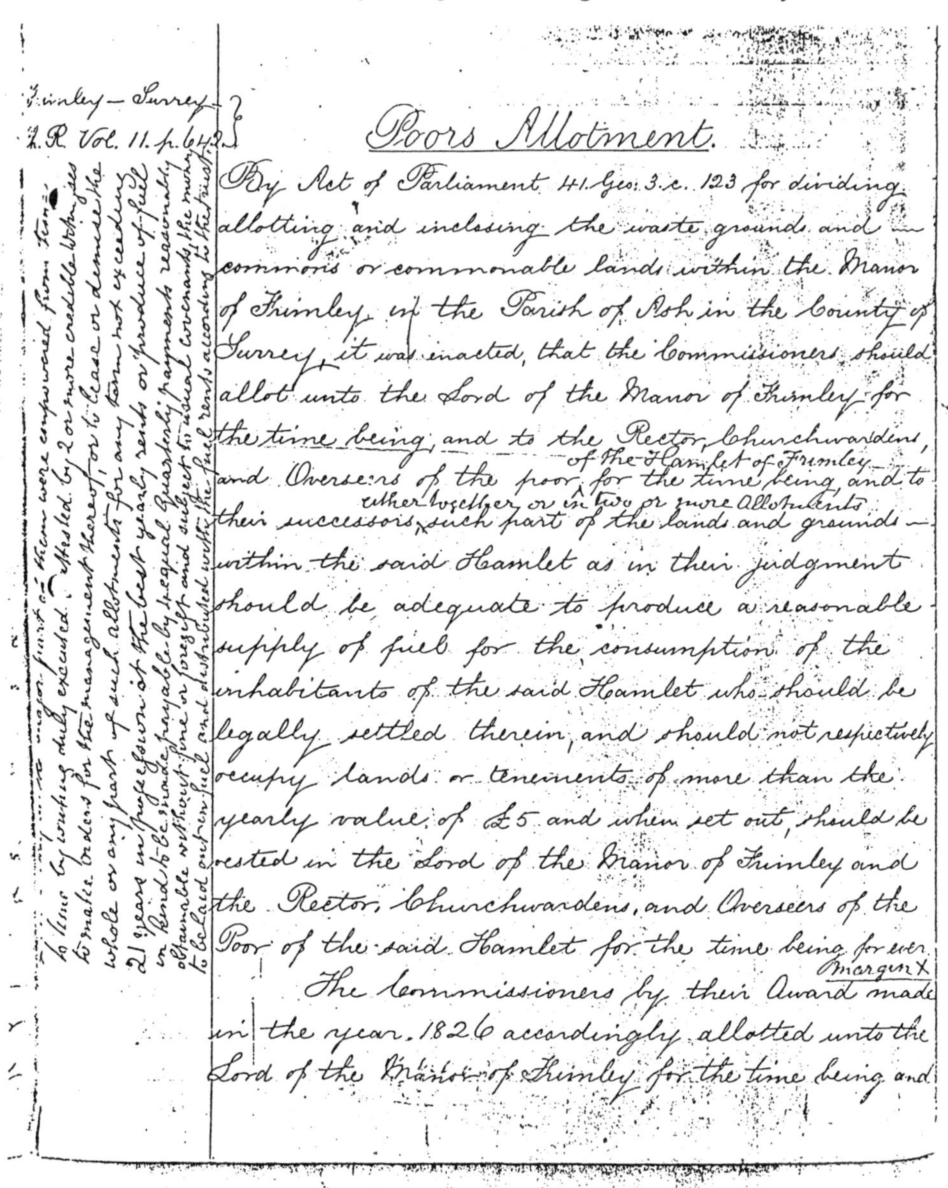

Frimley – Surrey
L.R. Vol. 11. p. 642.

Poors Allotment.

By Act of Parliament 41. Geo: 3. c. 123 for dividing, allotting and inclosing the waste grounds and commons or commonable lands within the Manor of Frimley in the Parish of Ash in the County of Surrey, it was enacted, that the Commissioners should allot unto the Lord of the Manor of Frimley for the time being, and to the Rector, Churchwardens, and Overseers of the poor of the Hamlet of Frimley for the time being, and to their successors, either together or in two or more Allotments, such part of the lands and grounds within the said Hamlet as in their judgment should be adequate to produce a reasonable supply of fuel for the consumption of the inhabitants of the said Hamlet who should be legally settled therein, and should not respectively occupy lands or tenements of more than the yearly value of £5 and when set out, should be vested in the Lord of the Manor of Frimley and the Rector, Churchwardens, and Overseers of the Poor of the said Hamlet for the time being for ever.

Margin X

The Commissioners by their Award made in the year 1826 accordingly allotted unto the Lord of the Manor of Frimley for the time being and

X ... the major part of them were empowered from time to time by writing duly executed & attested by 2 or more credible Witnesses to make orders for the management thereof, or to lease or demise the whole or any part of such allotments for any term not exceeding 21 years in possession at the best yearly rents or produce of fuel in Kind to be made payable by equal Quarterly payments reasonably obtainable without fine or foregift and subject to usual covenants, the money to be laid out in fuel and distributed with the fuel rents according to the trusts

The first Page of the Deed that established the Frimley Fuel Allotment.

CHAPTER 12

By the turn of the century Camberley had a population of 8,400. In 1901 King Edward VII came to the throne and the Victorian era ended.

It had been a period of almost unprecedented prosperity for many people and it could be truly said that the sun never set on any part of the world which was not a part of the British Empire. Huge markets for goods manufactured in Britain existed everywhere and our Industrial Revolution produced these in quantities hitherto thought to be impossible by the old methods of production. Railways had been built in profusion, motor cars were in their infancy, and the horse and cart was still the primary means of transport, together with the bicycle which had been invented in 1818.

Abroad in our Empire, merchant adventurers had made vast fortunes trading in commodities such as tea, sugar, coffee and jute. Our engineers constructed bridges, built railways and many beautiful buildings in foreign countries, especially in India. We had exported our legal system and our ideas of national Constitutions to the countries within our Empire and we supplied them with men to run their legislatures. Great plantations existed, particularly in the Far East, run by men from Britain.

We had a large Army stationed overseas, especially in India, where there had been periods of considerable unrest, one of which, the India Mutiny in 1857, had been very severe. This had resulted in the rule of India being taken over by the Crown from the East India Company and their private Company Army consisting of 38,000 Europeans and 350,000 Indians then became a part of the forces of the British Crown. In 1861 the Indian Staff Corps was formed to provide a body of officers for service in India and many other reforms were effected there between 1885 and 1904.

It was from India in particular, that men who had spent much of their life in the Indian Army or the Indian Civil Service, or who had made large fortunes in overseas trading enterprises, came to Camberley upon their retirement and built most of the 57 large houses that existed here in 1901, to form what was almost an ex-patriot Camberley community.

Why did they come here? The answer to this is two-fold. Firstly, some may have remembered the area from having been cadets at the R.M.C. or perhaps may have taken a course of study at the Staff College, but I think this can only have applied to a very few. What is far more likely is that it was an article that appeared in an Indian Military Magazine in 1875, that aroused the interest of wealthy men about to retire from India. This stated that large estates were available in a very healthy, heather and pine-clad countryside, completely unspoiled, within 1½ hour's train journey from London, and that the land was not expensive.

This must have sounded most attractive to men who had been living in parts of the Far East that were overcrowded, dry and barren. Many had been living in considerable state, in large houses, with innumerable servants, at no great cost to themselves, and upon retirement to England, hoped to find somewhere where conditions would allow them to continue to enjoy the life-style to which they had become accustomed.

But where might they find such a locality? Camberley must have seemed a likely place, and there must have also been a certain sense of nostalgia in

This was the India from which our new residents came, that of the British Raj. Above is the Taj Mahal at Agra. Built as a memorial to his beloved wife, Mumtaz Mahal, by the Moghul Emperor Shah Jehan in 1670, it is one of the most beautiful buildings in the world.

My father's regiment was stationed in India in the Punjab in World War 1 and the three photographs on this page were taken by him in 1919.
Above: The elephant procession of an Indian Rajah on his way to the River Ganges.
Left: Two snake charmers, who needless to say, have previously removed the poison sacs from the snakes.

the idea of living on a heather-clad moorland to those who had been starved of such scenery for so long.

And so they came, liked what they saw, bought the land and built their large houses here in Camberley. They also found that there were a considerable number of young women here who were glad of the opportunity to enter into domestic service in their houses, for there were few other avenues of employment open to many of them at that time. Men were also available to build their houses, tend their gardens, and look after their horses or motor cars. (For location of houses, see Maps, Page 37 and Page 112)

Many men who came here had known each other in India before settling in Camberley. Soldiers and sailors were of high rank, a number of whom had been knighted and considerably decorated during their years of service abroad, as had those who had been in the Indian Civil Service. They came in sufficient numbers to form a new aristocratic "Camberley society" of their own, amongst whom were included some other wealthy industrialists and professional men who also bought land and built houses here between 1880 - 1900.

One such was Mr G.W.Fowler, who, I am told, came from a family who had made a fortune as Chicago meat packers. He built Frimley Hall in 1882, but later sold this to Mr J.F.Wright, another industrialist, whose fortune came from the manufacture of soap and domestic boilers, and whose wife had been Miss Avery, a daughter of the family who manufactured the "Avery Scales" which were to be found in the kitchens of almost every housewife in the country. As well as the industrialists who had made their fortunes in Britain were some who had made theirs abroad, especially in the jute industry in India, such as Mr F.R.Charles the owner of "Clarewood" in the London Road, and Sir Robert Watson-Smyth who had "The Grove", near the Jolly Farmer Inn. Collingwood Secondary School now occupies his estate.

"Stockwood" in Crawley Hill Road, was the home of a very famous man, whose biography, like the Furse's of "Yockley House", is to be found in any encyclopedia. He was Colonel Charles Ryder C.B., C.I.E., D.S.O., who became the Surveyor-General of India. During his career, his work had become the basis of maps for the survey of India. In 1904 he headed the party sent to Lhasa to fix the boundaries of Tibet, and later surveyed 49,000 miles between Lhasa and British India, during which he established the height of Mount Everest. He was also the surveyor who established the boundaries between Turkey and Persia. His son was also famous and was awarded the V.C. for his part in the raid on St.Nazaire in World War II, a Combined Services Operation master-minded by Lord Louis Mountbatten.

Another renowned soldier who lived in Camberley was Lieutenant-General Sir Giffard Le Quesne Martel, who became well known as the authority on mechanisation and the employment of tanks in warfare, and commanded the 50th. Division in France in the early part of World War II. Later on, whilst at the War Office, I am told that he was instrumental in placing an order to produce some very hush-hush wooden panels of special design with the Camberley antique shop of Roberts in the High Street. It was only after the war was over it was discovered that these had been used to make wooden "dummy" tanks that were strewn about the fields of Kent as decoys should the Germans start to bomb our concentrations of war materials parked on open ground prior to the invasion of Europe.

Colonel W.E.Davies, who had "Heatherside House" in the 1920's after

Dr Leaf, had been present at the relief of Ladysmith in the Boer War. He had a wonderful collection of fine antique furniture, some of which he bequeathed to the Victoria and Albert Museum, who accepted this gift as the furniture was of the highest quality.

Major-General Sir W.Bird of "Glenturf" in the London Road was present at the siege of Mafeking and was awarded the D.S.O. He became A.D.C. to King George V in World War I and was a military historian on the strategy of the Russo-Japanese and Franco-Prussian wars. A point of interest about "Glenturf", which has now been turned into a block of flats, is that the Cam Stream flows underground through these estate grounds.

The legal profession had a number of distinguished representatives among "Camberley Society". Sir Harry Scott-Smith lived at "The Holt", Portsmouth Road, one of the oldest houses in Camberley still in existence. He had been a judge in the Punjab, and the Rt. Hon. Sir John Edge, whose home was "Waverley Court" had been the Chief Justice of the High Court in the N.W. Provinces of India. Sir Prior Goldney of "Prior Place" was the Recorder of Helston, and his brother, Sir Frederick Goldney, was the High Sherriff of Wiltshire.

As well as Lieutenant General Sir Giffard Martel, we had some other distinguished military engineers here in Camberley. Colonel Sir Henry McCallum of "Lauriston", Crawley Ridge, was the superintendent of Admiralty works responsible for the fortification of Singapore and Hong Kong around 1880, and afterwards became the Governor of Ceylon. Brigadier General F.H.Horniblow of "Summerhill", Crawley Hill, was the Chief Engineer of Malta in 1910. Sir John Carden, of "Carwarden House", Chobham Road, together with Captain V.Loyd of "Copped Hall" between them invented the Carden-Loyd tractor, which was afterwards used as the Bren-gun carrier in World War II. Sir John was keenly interested in the development of civil aviation but sadly, he was killed in a Dutch airliner crash in 1935. Another occupant of "Copped Hall" was Sir Harold Boulton, a well known lyricist and song writer. "Devon, Glorious Devon" was one of his best songs. He was also the organiser of the Bush Nursing Service in Australia and was a philanthropist to the poor in the East End of London.

A doctor was Major General Sir Menus O'Keefe, Col-Commandant of the R.A.M.C. in 1929, whose family were the publishers of the Belfast Telegraph. He lived at "Abbey Wood" in Park Road. Dr Rayner, who was a keen sportsman and President of the Camberley Football Club for many years, lived at "Harcourt House" in Frimley Road.

Amongst the diplomats was Sir Philip Currie of "Minley Manor" who was Lord Salisbury's Private Secretary in 1880, and himself Permanent Under-Secretary for Foreign Affairs in 1889. Sir Spencer St.John of "Pinewood Grange", London Road, accompanied Sir James Brooke to Borneo when he became the Rajah of Sarawak.

Bankers were also to be found among Camberley's distinguished residents. Sir Percy Newson, who lived at "Kingsclear" in the years before this house became a hotel and then later an Old Folks Home, had been the President of the Bank of Bengal, and Sir Alexander Roger, who was at "Yockley House" in 1930, was the Deputy Chairman of the Midland Bank.

In addition to Colonel Ryder's son we had two other soldiers who had been awarded the Victoria Cross. One was Major-General Sir Charles Mellis of "Five Trees", Tekels Avenue, who was decorated for his heroism at the relief of Kumasi in Ashanti, East Africa in 1900, and the other was Colonel Sir Arthur Hammond of "Sherborne House", Gordon Road, who was awarded his V.C. in the Afghan War of 1878.

Mr T.A.Ralli resided at Frimley Park Manor House in the 1920's. The Ralli family were cotton brokers from Liverpool, and both he and his family were prominent in many welfare activities in the town. They did much to improve the Manor House, constructing the sunken garden and formal gardens. The panelling in the Dining Room originally came from Chillingham Castle in Northumberland, and was installed at Frimley by Belgian craftsmen especially brought over to do the work. The House is now the centre for special training courses of about one week's duration for officers of the Cadet Corps throughout Britain.

"Old Dean Hall", a fine Tudor type house in the Branksome Park Road, was built by Mr G.W.Fowler after he sold Frimley Hall to Mr J.F.Wright. Later this house belonged to Mr B.Goodman. Like many others, he came to Camberley after leaving India, where he had been a bookmaker. It was said of him, by those who knew, that he would never let a young officer in India bet with him beyond his means and thus get into trouble. Mrs Goodman was very active in charitable events and fund-raising for many causes in the 1930's, and also during World War II, and Mr Goodman became the Conservative M.P for Islington.

THE AMPHIBIOUS TANK; ABLE TO CROSS RIVERS AND SPEED ACROSS ROUGH COUNTRY: THE CARDEN-LOYD TYPE, DEMONSTRATED IN 1931.

The Carden-Loyd Tank invented by Sir John Carden of Carwarden House, Upper Chobham Road, and Captain V.Loyd of Copped Hall, The Maultway.

CHAPTER 13

In the previous chapter I have tried to give my readers some idea of who the wealthy people were who composed "Camberley Society" in the 40 years which preceded World War II, and whose presence here provided many of the tradesmen of the town with their livelihoods, giving employment to many people in Camberley from 1899 - 1939.

One of these tradesmen was my father, who came here in 1909, and as I think a little of our family history may be of interest to my lady readers and will also help to paint the picture of what life was like in Camberley at that period, I have included this chapter in my book.

My father, Percy Wellard, was a Ladies' Hairdresser at Harrods in Knightsbridge, London, and came to Camberley in 1909. He opened our shop at 8 High Street in one of the oldest Camberley houses that still exists today. In Edwardian times, unlike today, only very wealthy ladies ever afforded themselves of the services of a ladies' hairdresser. Permanent waves were unknown, as was "setting" or "water-waving" the hair. Marcel waving, that is waving the hair with curling irons, by a method which had been invented by M.Marcel in Paris in 1852, comprised 50% of a ladies' hairdresser's work. The other half consisted of dressing long hair into elaborate shapes and adding false hair, or "postiche" as it was called, to enhance these "coiffures". This postiche was usually made in a back room on the hairdresser's premises and was a highly skilled process.

Outside of London Society there were few places existing in the provinces that had a sufficient number of wealthy ladies living in that locality to enable a ladies' hairdresser to make a livelihood there. A lady who lived in Camberley, and whose hair my father was dressing at Harrods in London in 1908, told him that she thought he would find enough clients in "Camberley Society" for him to be able to establish a Ladies' Hairdressing business here, and suggested that he should come down and look around to see what he thought of it. This he did, considered the outlook favourable, and found a small, gentlemen's hairdressing shop (combined with an umbrella repairers) was for sale in the High Street, bought it, married my mother and they arrived on Boxing Day after their honeymoon to open our shop in 1909. A postcard I have shows the previous owner, a gentlemen's hairdresser named Mr Andrews, standing in front of the shop in 1907, and I also have one of my mother standing in front of our shop during World War I in 1916, when my father was away serving in the army in India, and my mother was keeping our shop going during the war years.

When father started here he was the only Ladies' Hairdresser within a 15 mile radius. He spent much of his time travelling by bicycle to ladies' houses to wave and dress their hair for their house parties, and there were many of these going on in Camberley Society.

After World War I, soon after father returned to England, permanent waving was invented, utilising machines heated by electricity. But alas, there was no electricity in Camberley, and so in 1920 father had a special "Eugene" machine made which ran off accumulators, and he then did the first permanent wave in Camberley and district, which took all day. The lady who was brave enough to be father's first permanent wave customer was Mrs Williams, the wife of the dental surgeon who founded the practice at "Woodbourne" in Knoll Road. When electricity finally came to Camberley in

My mother in front of our shop in High Street. Taken in 1916 during the War Years when father was away in India.

Boating on the Basingstoke Canal and on the R.M.C. Lake was a favourite outing for many in Edwardian times.

1922, Mr Williams ran his electric drills, and father his permanent wave machine off the town's supply. But faults often occurred, and the supply failed and so whichever of the two was using electricity at the time would telephone the other to enquire whether it was his machine or the town's supply that had failed!

My own involvement with our family business did not commence until after World War II, when I took over upon my father's retirement in 1947. Like the sons in many other family businesses, I had been sent off in the 1930's to learn my profession in London. I worked in Regent Street first and then in Bond Street before World War II, when I joined the Navy which took me, like my father, to the Far East as well as the Mediterranean and Atlantic. The thing I remember most about those days was opening the gates of the prison, in which many civilians had been incarcerated for the war years, in Hong Kong to set them free again after the Japanese had left, and marvelling at the ingenuity the prisoners had displayed in adapting their lives to the ordeal they had had to face.

We had many distinguished ladies as clients of our salon during the 73 years of its existence, and I remember one in particular, not for the pleasure that her visits to my salon gave me, but the worry! She was the daughter of King Zog of Albania, who resided in this locality after he was deposed in World War II by the Italians. She used to chain-smoke the whole time, which was awkward enough for her hairdresser, but to add to this, she would never use an ash-tray, instead she used to fling lighted cigarettes that had been half-smoked on to the floor, expecting someone to pick them up. No doubt there were plenty to do so in her palace in Albania! One day, after one of her visits, we saw smoke coming through the ceiling of our shop from the salon above and, dashing upstairs, we found the rafters on fire. Fortunately, we managed to get it out before too much damage was done, and still more fortunately, the Princess soon afterwards left Camberley!

In father's time, a very famous man was a visitor to our salon - though not as a client! This was T.E.Lawrence of Arabia, who used to come to Camberley on his motor-cycle when he was stationed nearby, and meet a lady in our salon. He would sit and talk to her whilst she was having her hair done by my father. Lawrence mentioned this in his book, "The Seven Pillars of Wisdom".

In my attempts to research into the history of Camberley I have been helped enormously by the fact that, because of our family's long association with Camberley, so many people have been willing to talk to me, and to lend me valued documents connected with their past with which I have been enabled to construct the story of our town's early days. This is especially true in respect of the members of the Surrey Heath Local History Club and the Town's and R.M.A. Sandhurst's museum curators. Our family knew the lady members of many of the families who owned and lived in the large houses that I have written about, and who comprised the pre World War II "Camberley Society". All of them have been very willing to help me in my task of writing Camberley's history.

This is also true of the "military families" from the R.M.A.Sandhurst and the Staff College, who have so kindly assisted me. I have said before, that until 1950, when industry came to Camberley, that this was a military university town. Up until 1952 the townsfolk were able to walk or cycle through the beautiful "College" grounds, we could skate on the Staff College Lake in winter, and when I was young we could hire a boat for a picnic on the Lower Lake; it was also possible to get a pass to bathe in the R.M.C bathing lake. Just after World War II, when Major General F.Matthews and Major General Sir Hugh Stockwell were the Commandants, they made considerable efforts to bring "Town and Gown" closer together than they had been in the past. But alas, those days are gone! For about 1970, the need for security against terrorists, and the increased traffic due to the considerable housing developments surrounding the R.M.C., caused the R.M.A.S. grounds to be closed to the public, much to everyone's regret.

Pre World War II there were many restrictions on the cadets at Sandhurst. I remember that the cadets were only allowed into two of the tea shops in the town, Betty Brown's and the Mandarin, which was situated in the mid-part of the High Street. Strange to say, these two tea shops were also much frequented by some of the attractive daughters of the townsfolk too, and I am sure that quite a few of the Army wives of today remember just where their romances started in those way-off days! Cadets were not able to go into any public house closer to the R.M.C. than Bagshot or the "Ely" on Hartford Bridge Flats. When their parents visited them they were only allowed to lunch with them at the Duke of York or the Cambridge Hotel. Those of the cadets who had cars, and the King of Jordan was one of these, had to keep them in garages outside the College grounds.

Any young lady from the town whom a cadet wished to invite to the June Sovereign's Parade Ball had to be introduced beforehand to the cadets' divisional officer. And what a marvellous affair that Ball was! Dinner in the mess preceded it. Three or four huge marquees were set up in the grounds, top London bands were engaged and one would find Joe Loss playing in one marquee, and the Kinsmen in another. All the girls had really lovely dresses and the cadets proudly wore their new lieutenant's uniform. At the end of a very long night, there was breakfast, and hopefully it was all accompanied by glorious June weather.

They were certainly something to remember, bringing happy nostalgic memories to many in the sad days of the war that followed. To the townsfolk, the most enduring memory that many of us carry is that of being able to witness the "Passing Out Parades", with their fine ceremonial, especially the moment when the Adjutant on his horse disappeared through the doors of Old College behind the battalion of young officers who had just received their commissions. Another memorable event to which we were occasionally invited was the "Beating the Retreat" ceremony at eventide. Such were the things that made we townsfolk proud to have the R.M.C. here amongst us in our town of Camberley.

The Sovereign's Parade. The Queen is to be seen inspecting the Parade at the left centre of this picture.

CHAPTER 14

In 1869 Captain Raleigh Knight put up part of his land, the "Tekells Castle Estate" of 333 acres, for sale by private treaty. This comprised all that area now bounded by Heatherdale Road and Pine Avenue on the west, Portsmouth Road on the south, Park Road on the north and Church Hill/Crawley Hill on the east. He offered this as one lot, but stated that additional land could also be purchased if so desired, or alternatively that he was prepared to reduce the acreage. (Maps, Page 36 and Page 37)

General Byrne, who had previously been a tenant of his in Tekells Castle, bought the whole estate. At the time of the sale Mrs Fitzpatrick was living in the Castle with a lease that expired in 1875, after which General Byrne was able to gain full possession of the estate and he then lived at the Castle until his death in 1898.

In 1892 he decided to split his estate into four parts, which he named Tekells Castle Estate, Brackendale Estate, Waverley Estate and Pine Woods Estate. He kept Tekells Castle himself and offered the other three estates for sale by auction, and this attracted a number of gentlemen who lived in or around Bournemouth. Possibly their interest in Camberley had been aroused by an article that had appeared in the "Lancet" in 1883, extolling the very healthy climate of our pine clad area, which was similar in many respects to that of Bournemouth. Certainly they foresaw its considerable attraction to wealthy men who might be seeking retirement homes.

Amongst the land speculators who came to the sale were Mr James Page and Mr Maurice Lawson, of whom more in a later chapter. A firm of estate agents, Messrs Hankinson, bought the Brackendale Estate, and the Waverley Estate was purchased by them on behalf of Mr T.D.Edwardes. The Pine Woods Estate, which comprised the Belton Road area, was sold in 1892 to Mr E.B.Walker, who came from Parkstone in Dorset. He then divided it into three parts, retaining the area which later became Belton Road and Walkers Ridge himself, and also another small estate of about 10 acres in which he built "Tekells House", later called "Brooks Court" when occupied by General Brooke Chambers. The third part was sold to Mr H.Balfour, who built "Belton" there. Bellever Hill and Deepwell Drive now occupy this area.

Mr Walker put up his "Pine Woods Estate", now much reduced in size, for sale in January 1898, divided into 36 building plots. The prospectus stated that "this Building Land is situated on a spur of the Surrey Hills, half a mile from Camberley Station and is surrounded by large properties owned by wealthy owners and is suitable for the erection of houses of from £60 to £150 per annum (Presumably "to let"). Water will be laid on and the New Roads finished by about September 1898". The roads shown on the plan were Belton Road and Waverley Road, (the latter being re-named Grange Road and Walkers Ridge afterwards). But, for some reason, there were only 3 small houses built in Belton Road between 1898 and 1914, and it was not until after World War I that this estate showed any further development.

By 1895 two houses had been built on the neighbouring Waverley Estate. The first of these was "Waverley Court", which occupied a beautiful site near the summit of Crawley Hill where there had formerly been a Keeper's cottage with an orchard. This was now transformed into the pleasure gardens of an elegant Edwardian house which had balconies leading out from its first floor bedrooms, a sheltered patio in front of the house and a rounded tower

Brackendale Estate in 1898 before any houses were built there. Practically the whole of Camberley's residential area was like this before housing development commenced.

The main entrance lodge to Captain Knight's Tekells Castle Estate. Afterwards, this drive became Heatherdale Road when the Brackendale Estate started to be built.

Waverley Court, near the crest of Church Hill. The estate is now Red Crest Gardens. Sir John Edge, a Chief Justice of the High Court in the N.W. Provinces of India, once lived there.

The house was set in several acres of woodland.

Left: Yapton, the front entrance with the Thomas family crest above the door.

The Thomas family came from Yapton in Sussex and a Baronetcy was granted to them by King George III for services in the American Colonies before the Declaration of Independence and the Revolutionary War. The title is now extinct. The house was situated in Brackendale Road near to Beech Avenue and had a croquet lawn, a formal garden and a tennis court.

on the corner of the building, showing that Mr Poulter was the building's architect! The terraced gardens led down to a tennis court and below this there was another terraced croquet lawn with a monkey puzzle tree. Altogether the house and grounds occupied a 10 acre estate. This house has now been demolished and the very pleasant houses along Redcrest Gardens have been built on this estate. Fortunately quite a few of the beautiful trees have been preserved to help one to picture what a fine house "Waverley Court" must have been in its heyday.

The other house, "The Holt", has survived to this day. It is situated about 50 yards to the west of the Ravenswood cross roads roundabout over the M3, alongside the Old Portsmouth Road, in the cul-de-sac formed when that road was diverted. Originally the grounds of "The Holt" stretched back from the Portsmouth Road to Claremont Avenue, and the Watchetts Stream started here before continuing on through the Tekells Castle Estate. In 1920 this house was owned by Sir Harry Scott-Smith and, at the same time, Sir John Edge resided at "Waverley Court"; both were judges from the N.W. of India and, no doubt, knew each other before retiring to Camberley.

From 1900 onwards first Waverley Drive was constructed through the centre of the Waverley Estate, and then two side roads were added, Castle Road and Connaught Road. By 1907 there were 11 houses in these roads, but this number had increased to 38 by 1913, and no more building plots were available. Two further side roads were then constructed, Grove Road and Claremont Avenue, but these were not built upon until after World War I ended in 1918. Of the 38 houses on the Waverley Estate in 1913, 3 were owned by Knights, and there was an Admiral, a General, 9 Colonels, 2 Majors, 9 Captains, 1 Parson and only 12 civilians, some of whom were the widows of officers, on this estate.

The Brackendale Estate was advertised for building development in 1898, an attractive brochure being produced by Messrs. Sadler and Baker, the estate agents, for this purpose. This contained pictures of some of the streets in Camberley and Yorktown, and of some of the large houses existing at that time, stressing the aristocratic nature of their owners. It is indeed by far the most authoratitive pictorial record of our town at the turn of the century, and I count myself fortunate to have a copy of this in my possession. Photographs of the land available for building on the estate show Brackendale to have been a site of great beauty, with a drive into the estate lined with rhododendron bushes. This had, at one time, been the main drive leading to Tekells Castle, with a gate across the road and a lodge nearby. It now became Heatherdale Road, the first road on the Brackendale Estate to be developed. This was then continued southwards as Pine Avenue towards the Portsmouth Road, and these two roads marked the estate border with the Watchetts, the development of which did not commence until 1929.

A number of large houses were built around 1885 in Pine Avenue and also nearby in Heatherdale Road, all on plots of between 3-5 acres. Amongst these was "Holcombe House" ("Cavendish House") now the home of Colonel Shepperd, the distinguished historian, who wrote the authoratitive book on "Sandhurst" from which I have quoted in Chapter 3 (with his permission). He was the librarian at the R.M.A. for many years after World War II, and both he and his charming wife have done much to assist the mentally handicapped charities in the district for many years. By 1913 all 16 plots in Heatherdale Road had been sold and 4 of the 5 plots in Pine Avenue. These were all on the eastern side of Pine Avenue as its western side was in the Watchetts Estate. The "Kingsclear" estate bordered about half of Heatherdale Road and this was not developed until the 1960's.

CAMBERLEY 1913

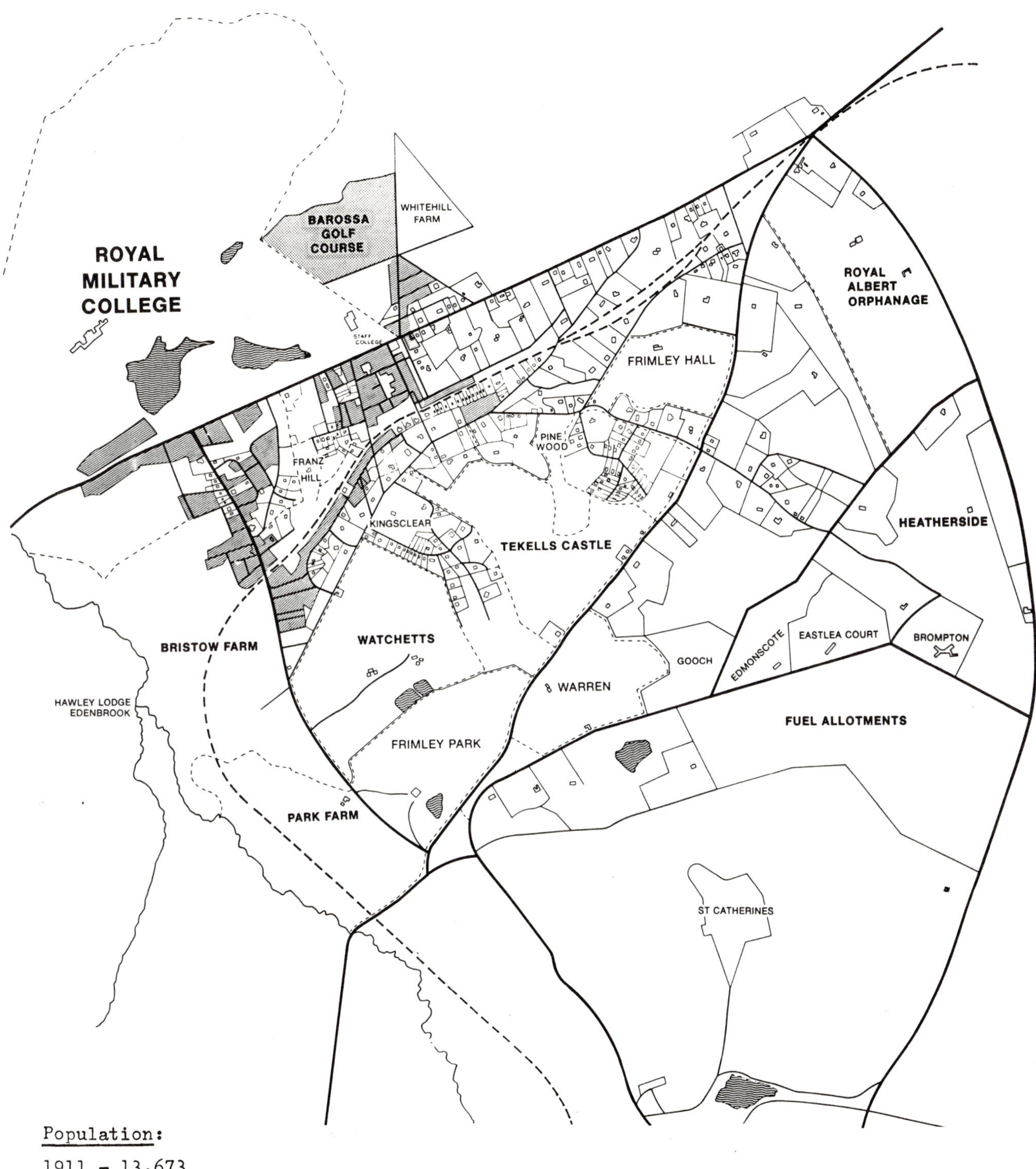

Population:

1911 - 13,673

By 1913 much further development had occurred on the Woodlands Estate and the area alongside Gordon Road had been built up. Smaller houses had been erected on both sides of Frimley Road and along several new roads that led towards the Peat Moor. In 1908 the Franzhill Estate was sold and development started along Southwell Park Road. The Brackendale and Waverley Estates which had commenced their development programmes in 1898 were 2/3rds built up by 1914. The construction of Camberley Heath Golf course started in 1912 but was not opened until 1st. January 1914.

"Kingsclear" was built about 1890 by Mr Charles C.King, who named the house after himself, spelling it "Kingsclere". In 1901 it was sold to Captain C.R.Knight's son, Henry, who rented it to a number of tenants.

It then became the home of Mr W.R.Davies, who was a J.P., and keenly interested in the sporting clubs of Camberley, being President of the football club after World War I, and also a member of the golf club. Later the house belonged to Sir Percy Newson and, after his death, it was bought by Mr Maurice Lawson, the brother-in-law of Mr James Page. Mr Lawson was a very fine cricketer, an opening batsman, who had played for Hampshire as an amateur. He was an architect, also a hotel owner and, in 1950, had the Camberley Court Hotel (previously "Firlands House" in Park Road, which was managed by his son, Howard. He now turned "Kingsclear" into a very expensive and exclusive hotel with a Swiss manageress, but it was not successful. It remained empty for a time and then, largely due to the fund-raising efforts of Camberley's Rotary Club, together with a money grant from the Council, it was purchased to found Kingsclear "Old Folks Home", which it is today.

Some 50% of the original Kingclear Estate was sold for building in order to augment the sum required for this, and since then the Home has received much fund-raising assistance from the Rotary Club, the Round Table and the Lions Club to help with its maintenance. It now cares for 68 old people, 24 of whom are nursing home cases living in two specially built wings of the Home.

To return to 1898. By the eastern side of the Kingsclear Estate, another drive led to the Tekells Castle Estate (which was to become Tekells Avenue in 1920). The first part of Brackendale Road was now made alongside this drive, from which it continued on through the middle of the Brackendale Estate with Pinemount Road, Beech Road and Norwich Avenue branching off towards the Tekells Estate.

By 1907, 3 large houses, "Roscommon", "Yapton" and "Beechleigh", had been built in Brackendale Road as well as 5 smaller ones. "Astolat" was in Beech Avenue, and "Derramore", "Ingle Dell" and "Rathfarnham" in Pinemount Road. The latter was the home of Sir George Grierson, a linguistic expert in Hindustani, Sanskrit and other Oriental languages.

One of Camberley's most famous sporting personalities, Miss Molly Gourlay, lives in Brackendale Road. She was English Golf Champion in 1926 & 1929 and won many big tournaments before becoming President of the E.L.G.U. 1957-1960.

Another famous Camberley sporting lady, Miss M.Maclagan, lives in Heathcote Road. She achieved fame playing cricket for the English Ladies team against Australia and New Zealand in the 1930's as an opening bat and bowler. And today, another lady, Miss Maxine Burton, is carrying on the good work in the ladies professional golfing world.

Altogether the residential developments that took place in Camberley between the years 1891 and 1911 increased the town's population from 5,295 to 13,673.

and, no doubt, his firm has played a considerable part in all the developments that took place here in the years that followed, and has so altered it from the muddy little village that he found in 1881!

The second railway line was laid in the early 1900s.

Camberley High Street 1901. Princess Street on the left. Several of the houses built in the fields on the right had by then been turned into shops.

View of the High Street with Obelisk Steeet corner on the right. Evans the Chemists became Boots and is now the Halifax Building Society.

The London Road, near to the High Street corner. Pank's Emporium, an old-fashioned household utensil store and ironmongers. Next to this was a stationers and booksellers, D.Norman, who became the town's first Postmaster, in the Post Office built next to him. Beyond, in the distance can be seen the Inn Sign outside the Staff Hotel. Circa 1898.

The Staff Hotel, 1906. One of the signs outside reads: "Staff Livery & Bait Stables": Good loose boxes for Hunters & Polo Ponies: H.Young Proprietress": Mrs Young is standing outside the front door of the hotel. Another sign reads: "ER" Recruits are now wanted for all branches of His Majesty's Army: God Save The King:" (King Edward VII)

Original Frimley and Camberley U.D.C. Offices in London Road. Built on land that was once a Nursery Garden. To the left of the Municipal Building can be seen Appley House, a villa that had by then become the Victoria Hotel. The row of semi-detached houses beyond, that had been turned into shops, is Appley Place.

St.Michaels, built 1851 on ground presented to the Church by the R.M.C. On the opposite side of London Road are some of the early shops in Yorktown on Osnaburgh Hill.

CHAPTER 16

In 1894 the "Urban District of Frimley" Council was set up. Its domain covered an area of 12 square miles, comprising Frimley, Camberley, Frimley Green, Deepcut and Mytchett. (i.e. the Tichborne's original Frimley Manor, plus the land added to this by the 1801 Frimley Enclosure Act).

At first the Council consisted of 15 members, but later expanded to include 3 more. The population of Camberley and Yorktown was then about 6,000, but by 1914 when World War I commenced it had grown to almost 13,500. The Council purchased a portion of the Franzhill Estate that had once been known as "Tough's Nursery" on which they built the Municipal Offices facing the London Road in 1906, and turned the rest of the land into London Road Recreation Ground, building the pavilion in 1898. N.B. John Tough Finch, the son of John Tough, was one of the early convict-settlers of Australia. Transported in 1837 after being court martialled for going AWOL from the British Army, he was assigned as shoemaker to Major General Stewart.

Upon receiving his freedom 7 years later he married Ann Meredith, a Welsh girl who had emigrated there on an assisted passage. Eventually they became farmers and settled in Garra, having adopted the surname of Bennett. Their family history is now in the Australian National Library.

Running along the side of the "Rec" was Grand Avenue, a private road which was the entrance drive to the Franzhill Estate (of which "Firwood" was a part and the farmlands of New Farm) and, since Viscount Southwell owned it, was also known as Southwell Park. The Estate had originally occupied the whole area bounded by the railway, The Avenue, London Road and Park Street but, in addition to the part sold to the Council, another portion (which is now the Charles Street car park) had been sold to Mr George Doman in 1897 and Captain H.R.Knight had also built some cottage type houses with gardens along the west side of Park Street.

In 1908 the estate of 42 acres was put up for sale by auction; it then had two houses on it, "Franzhill House" and "Firwood". The plan of the estate had 3 "Suggested Roads", the first of which was a continuation of Grand Avenue southwards until it almost reached the railway (this was re-sited a little to the west when it was eventually made and became France Hill Drive). The second road suggested became Firwood Drive and the third, Southwell Park Road, joining The Avenue to Park Street.

However, the reserve of £14,000 for the whole estate was not reached at the auction, and it was afterwards sold privately to a syndicate of Camberley business men amongst whom I surmise was my old landlord, Mr Pank, who had the ironmongery store "Pank's Emporium", Mr Doman, who had livery stables in Yorktown, and Mr Sparvell, who had a bakery and grocer's business in Camberley in 1911.

By 1913 a start had been made on the development of the estate and the roads constructed. Two or three houses were built at the start of Firwood Drive on its eastern side, but then the war came. Meanwhile "Franzhill House" and all the land between France Hill Drive and The Avenue had been sold to Mrs Forbes, who probably was the one who now called it "France Hill House", owing to the anti-German feelings aroused during World War I when anyone with a name which could be remotely thought of as German promptly anglicised it, (e.g. Prince Louis Battenburg - who changed his name to

Mountbatten). The further development of Firwood Drive and the eastern side of France Hill Drive was recommenced in 1918 together with Southwell Park Road, and by 1939 there were only one or two plots still left in all 3 roads. (1913 Map, Page 67 and 1938 Map, Page 93)

On the neighbouring Woodlands Estate development had been more rapid. In 1898 there were only 7 houses on the eastern side of The Avenue set in building plots of about 1-1½ acres, and 7 houses on smaller plots between Heatherley Road and Woodlands Road. By 1913 there were 24 on the eastern side of The Avenue and 12 on the western and 20 houses ran along Woodlands Road.

In 1910 a cinema appeared in Camberley's High Street. This was located in a house that had been built in 1870 and later turned into a draper's shop by Mr James Page when he first came to Camberley around 1900. I am told that in 1910 he sold this building to Mr Alfred Ashby, another High Street draper, who turned it into the "Electric" cinema and installed Mr Brett there as manager. Mr Page then moved up the road to open a new Department Store on the Obelisk Street/High Street corner, in what had previously been known as the "Lords" house.

About the same time that my father founded our hairdressing salon in 1909, four other "family dynasty" businesses were also being started here. Mr Percy White was turning his cycle and sewing machine shop into a motor garage and Mr Herman Solomon his motorbicycle shop into a motor car salesroom and garage. He began his enterprise in the premises next door to "The Crockery" in the High Street opposite to our shop, and outside his garage there used to stand a row of Ford "Tin Lizzies" waiting for sale. My father bought one in 1920 and we had many fine outings in this "open" motor car, in which my mother sat, clad in a leather motoring coat with a large veil over her hat and face, to protect her from the wind and the dust from the gravelly roads as we bowled along the countryside on our way to the seaside.

Another family firm which lasted for 75 years, as did ours, was J.F.Hawkins, the gentlemen's outfitters, in the middle part of the High Street. Mr Hawkins believed in advertising, and many old brochures or street maps of Camberley carry his firm's advertisements.

The Home Farm on Heatherside was the starting point for Mr F.Stokes' dairy firm. He also had a shop in Park Street where he sold his produce as well as delivering milk with his horse and cart, all of which came direct from his farm. Now the firm has large premises in Pembroke Way, with almost a monopoly of the dairy business in Camberley, and it is still being run by the Stokes family. Miss Mona Stokes married Mr Richard White to unite these two old Camberley business families and their son, Peter, carries on the "Whites" garage firm, now expanded into other fields as well.

By 1913 the Frimley Road had become lined with houses stretching from the bridge over the railway northwards to the London Road. The William IV Inn, which had been built in 1853, was conveniently situated close to Moorlands Road and Vale Road which led on to the Peat Moor. It was also close to the fields of Bristow Farm to the west of Frimley Road. No doubt this was very handy for the farm labourers on a hot and thirsty day!

The development of this part of Yorktown is also bound up with another family who played a prominent role in the town's pre World War II history. They were the Doman brothers, who came to Camberley from Basingstoke about

The High Street about 1925. The "Lord's House" which became James Page's Department Store is seen in the centre of the picture, with the shop fronts that he added to the original building. The circularly domed glass building next to it was the conservatory in which Mr Craig used to sell the products from his Nursery Garden, which was behind. Box & Gillhams later became Lloyds Bank and the villa and the row of five semi-detached houses built from the Obelisk Street corner towards the station can also be seen. The Electric Cinema is the taller building just beyond these. Our shop was to the right of Box & Gillhams, which was built on what was the Nursery Garden in 1870.

The London Road premises of Overs Store decorated for the coronation of King Edward VII in 1902. He visited Camberley in 1905 and toured the town by car. These premises were gutted by fire in 1907 and rebuilt.

"Tin Lizzies" standing outside Herman solomon's original showrooms in the High Street. These were almost opposite to my old High Street shop. The Crockery Shop occupies these premises now. The garden to the left is where Woolworths has been built.

The Electric Cinema in the High Street. Converted from a draper's shop in 1910, it was Camberley's first cinema. The lettering of the word cinema can still be seen on the side wall of the toy shop, which it is today.

1890. George Doman started as a dairyman in a shop on the corner of London Road and Victoria Avenue, which was just a short lane then. Very soon he opened a livery stable which was much used by the Sandhurst cadets. Amongst these was Winston Churchill, who kept his horses there whilst he was at the R.M.C.

When the telephone service first started about 1900, George, who was an enterprising chap, immediately installed one. His number was Camberley 2. He expanded his business by inaugurating a horse-bus service in the town, and then bought land in the now extended Victoria Avenue. He gave this to the Council for them to build Council Houses there. He then built some houses himself in Edward Avenue and Alexandra Avenue nearby, with the intention of letting them. Meanwhile, he had become a member of the new Town Council and, upon becoming its Chairman, took a great interest in the provision of some recreational facilities for young people. In 1914 he decided to go into the new cinema industry, and built Camberley's second cinema not far away from the Duke of York hotel, calling this the "Academy".

A few years previously, his sister had married Mr H.W.Fairs, who was the Racquets professional at the R.M.C. (a form of Squash as we know it today). During World War I, he ran a taxi service for cadets from a garage in the Frimley Road, but after the war he left the R.M.C. and went into the cinema business too, with his brother-in-law as partner. They opened the "Arcade" cinema almost opposite to the Staff College gates. However, this hit business at the "Academy" in Yorktown, and it closed soon afterwards.

To the rear of the cinema was the Peat Moor, an area of some 25 acres which stretched from Victoria Avenue westwards to the Blackwater River. In 1819 this belonged to James Seaton, who gave it to the "Governors of the Bounty of Queen Anne", a church trust. The Governors of the Trust were appointed by the Bishop of the Diocese, and in the 1920's, Canon Partridge of St.Peters, Frimley, was one of these. In 1928 they sold the Peat Moor to George Doman, but nothing was done with the land until it was sold to the Camberley Sand and Gravel Company in 1942. Then, in 1949, it was acquired by the Frimley and Camberley Urban District Council in order to provide a site for the "Yorktown Industrial Estate", the first few factories appearing there several years later.

King Edward VII visiting Camberley in June, 1905

CHAPTER 17

Bristow Farm is by far the most ancient part of Camberley. It dates back to the reign of Henry III when it was called Burstowe, which means "a fortified place" and, as the present farmhouse was at one time surrounded by a small moat, it may once have been used as a small fort to prevent enemy invasion across the Blackwater River.

In 1569 Thomas and Richard Bristowe were tenants of the Tichborne family who owned the farm as part of their Frimley Manor. In 1669 their tenant was Sir Thomas Foote, and in 1686 Mr Morgan Randyll. Mr Robert Jennens held the farm in trust for John Churchill, first Duke of Marlborough in 1714, but four years later, by direction of Sir James Tichborne, it was transferred to Joseph and George Musgrave. In 1776 Bristowe was known as Hind Coppice but in 1790 it was sold to Mr James Laurell when he bought Frimley Manor from the Tichbornes. It then passed to John Tekell and to Captain Raleigh Knight's brother-in-law, Major R.Spring.

In 1869 the farm was purchased by John Hollings of Wheatley Hall, Bradford, at the same time that he purchased part of the Watchetts lands. In 1884 John Hollings died and his son, "Squire" H.J.B.Hollings succeeded to the property. "H.J.B." married Nina, the daughter of General Smyth who resided at "Frimhurst", a large estate beside the Basingstoke Canal in Frimley Green (later a country club which Prince Aly Khan and Rita Hayworth, the film actress, used to visit).

Her sister was Dame Ethel Smyth the famous composer, who lived at "One Oak" on the Portsmouth Road, now an Inn. She was a most interesting lady. Born in 1858, she composed hymns as a child. After a musical education at Leipzig, she commenced to compose and her most famous work, Mass in D, was performed at the Albert Hall in 1893, and in 1910 her opera, The Wreckers, became the first opera by a woman to be performed at Covent Garden. She was a friend of the Empress Eugenie who was living at Farnborough Mount (now Farnborough Hill School) in 1887. A woman of great energy, she became a militant Suffragette, spending two months in Holloway prison in 1913 for her part in their activities. Amongst friends who visited her at "One Oak" were Sir Thomas Beecham, George Bernard Shaw and Keir Hardy, a founder of the Labour Party. She was made a D.B.E. in 1922.

Squire Hollings also owned Hacklane Farm on the Watchetts Estate as well as Bristowe, and so in addition to being a barrister by profession, he was a farmer in a considerable way, and employed more than 20 men on his farms. He took a great interest in all that was going on in Camberley, particularly in its sporting activities, and was also a Justice of the Peace. He died in 1922 when the whole of his estate was bought by Mr Verran, of whom more later.

Frimley Park Farm, to the south of Bristowe, was farmed by George Hills in the years prior to World War I. He had been Captain Knight's Resident Manager of the Tekells Castle Estate until it was sold, whereupon Captain Knight installed him on Park Farm as his tenant. George Hills was a fine man and was for many years an Urban District Councillor. He retired in 1912 when Captain Knight sold the farm to Mr J.Fowles, who had a butcher's shop in Yorktown, and his son, who had learned farming under Mr Hills, took over the farm. Mr Hills died in 1925.

By 1913 Captain C.R.Knight's son, Henry (H.R.) who had inherited his father's remaining property in Camberley, had sold the last four building plots that lay between London Road, Camberley and the railway to the east of High Street. "St Anns", a beautiful half timbered house, was built for Colonel Lushington and still exists today. "Carlinwark", Colonel Lidderdale's home, was next to "Crosby Hall", the home of the Muller family who were associated with the giant German chemical firm of Ludwig Mond. "Pinewood Grange", (now Larchwood Glade) was built for Sir Spencer St.John, the diplomat who went to Sarawak with Brooke, and the other house built there was "The Wirral". This was also known as "Eastfields" and Major General Sir Charles Knowles, who was present at the fall of Sebastopol in the Crimean War, lived there. He had known Cambridge Town in its early days as he had graduated at the Staff College only 2 years after it had opened in 1862. (Map, Page 112 for location of houses)

South of the railway in Crawley Ridge Road three notable houses were built. "Old Dean Hall" (now "Tudor Hall" flats) was originally owned by Mr G.W.Fowler who moved there after he had built "Frimley Hall" and sold it to Mr J.F.Wright. It is said that he much regretted having parted with this, and tried to buy it back from Mr Wright with no success, and so he built "Old Dean Hall" nearby so that he could overlook his old "Frimley Hall" estate.

In the years immediately preceding World War I, Colonel Chesyre Walker was at "Wargrave House" next door, but just after the war he sold it to Admiral Sturdee, of the "Battle of the Falklands" in World War I fame, in which he inflicted a crushing defeat upon the German Cruiser squadrons of Von Spee. After the war Admiral Sturdee was largely responsible for the restoration of Nelson's flagship H.M.S.Victory at Portsmouth. He was made an Admiral of the Fleet in 1921, and when he died in 1925 he was given a State Funeral in Camberley. An eye-witness at his funeral told me that the coffin was on a gun-carriage pulled by naval ratings, and present were representatives of all the services, both military and civil. The funeral service was held at St Pauls, Crawley Hill, where he used to read the lessons, followed by burial at St Peters, Frimley. The procession was so long that the head of it had reached St Peters, about 1½ miles away, before the tail of the procession had left St Pauls. It was a truly magnificent spectacle, never to be forgotten by all who saw it. A wooden cross, made from the timbers of H.M.S.Victory by the shipwrights who restored her under Admiral Sturdee's direction, is erected over his tomb in the churchyard.

"The Ridge" was owned by another naval officer, Captain Lowther R.N., and was next door to "Wargrave House". Ashwell Avenue now occupies the estates of these two houses, and I am surprised that this road was not named to commemorate the naval connection of such a famous man as Admiral of the Fleet Sturdee. However, there is a Sturdee Close in Frimley not far from where he is buried.

In Frimley, south of the Chobham Road, "Oak Lea", later re-named "Athallan Grange", had been built about 1890. It was originally occupied by Mrs Lyne, but about 1907 it became the home of Mrs Spens who had previously lived at "Frimley Park". She was a great huntswoman, and one morning she and one of her sons were out hunting and somehow got out on to the Army Ranges at Ash, where Bobbie was accidentally shot and killed. He is buried in Frimley churchyard. Today "Athallan Grange" has been demolished and the Marconi factory occupies the site.

Next to "Athallan" was "Alphington" which originally belonged to an

American family named Furse (probably related to Charles Wellington Furse who lived in "Yockley House"), but in 1914 it was owned by Brigadier General W.D.Findlay who was killed at Mons only a few days after the commencement of World War I. On the other side of "Athallan" was "Grovefield" where Mr W.J.Burrell, the Lord of the Manor, lived with his sister, Mrs Fry. Their family gave Frimley Grove green to the F.& C.U.D.Council in the 1930's to be preserved as a public open space.

The "Alphington" Estate has now become the Tomlins Housing Estate and Tomlinscote School stands on the site of "Tomlinscote House". It had a large orchard and was occupied by Mr H.Bidwell and his unmarried sister, who used to breed a small type of dog called a "Dandy Dinmont". In my schoolboy days, when I was learning to play golf on Barossa Golf Course, I well remember an old gentleman, Colonel Lodwick, who was nearly blind being accompanied round by two of these little dogs who used to find his ball for him. Barossa Golf Course, constructed on Barossa Farm, had started up in 1903 and carried on until 1940, when it was sold to the Staff College to become their playing fields.

Tomlins Pond, and the area immediately surrounding it, was in an estate of beautifully wooded land known as "Frimley Court". There was only one house on the estate "Tomlins Cottage", described in the estate sale particulars in 1902 as a "quaint eight-roomed Lodge at the entrance from Chobham Road". It was then occupied by Mr Tarrant, a builder who had built "Roscommon" in Brackendale Road among other large houses. His wife gave piano lessons, one of her pupils being Daisy Hills. In those days the Frimley Stream coming down from Jackpond Hill ran in to Tomlins Pond and thence through a pen-stock, which controlled its rate of flow, over a waterfall into the smaller lake next door in "Alphington". Early in 1920 this pen-stock was pulled out by mischievous boys, or else it gave way, and the water poured out from the lakes at great speed along its old course to Frimley village where it flooded Frimley Street feet deep, and also many of the houses there, causing quite a sensation!

In Frimley village, situated near to the White Hart Inn, was "The Priory" which was first owned by Fitzroy H.Somerset, and then by Colonel Faithful. Later this became a restaurant called "Priors Kitchen", and was run by Miss H.Mason. It was later pulled down and a parade of shops with a car park behind now occupies the grounds of "The Priory".

"Manor House" was opposite to St.Peters Church and was the home of the Lord of the Manor who, in 1873, was Mr J.F.Burrell. It is somewhat confusing to talk of the "Frimley Park Manor House" and of another "Manor House" in Frimley. I will try to simplify matters. The Lord of the Manor, owner of Frimley's "Manor House", Mr Burrell, only owned land to the <u>south</u> of Chobham Road, that is land between Frimley and Frimley Green, and did <u>not</u> own any land to the north of this, and after Frimley Manor was split up in 1806 the land to the <u>north</u> of Portsmouth Road was called the "Frimley Park Estate" (now Camberley), whose ownership and history I have been describing in previous chapters, and this contained the original Frimley Manor House built by Sir James Tichborne. Mr Burrell and Mr Kingdom bought their land after James Laurell's death around 1865. Captain C.R.Knight bought his after the death of John Tekell in 1858, but the title of Lord of the Manor did not go with this. Instead it went with the land sold to Mr Burrell by the widow of James Laurell, the previous Lord of the Manor, in 1872, and consisted of Frimley village and the tenant farms to the south of this.

The house that Mr Burrell then occupied in Frimley village was thereafter called "Manor House" and the Frimley Manor House, "Frimley Park Manor House". In all he owned 276 acres of the original Frimley Manor Estate in 1886, and Mr A.C.Pain, of St.Catherines, who had also purchased some of the Manor lands, had 202 acres in 1893.

THE SURREY BORDER AND CAMBERLEY RAILWAY

The Miniature Railway that ran from Frimley to Yorktown through Park Farm and Bristow Farm in 1939.

The floods in Frimley Steet after the pen-stock of the pond in "Alphington" had been removed in 1920.

CHAPTER 18

Camberley Heath Golf Course is sited in Cart Bottom along the Frimley Ridge, half of it being in Collingwood Park and the other half lying between this and the Warren Estate on the land enclosed by Thomas Knight in 1801. In 1912-13 when the Golf Course was constructed, this area was a heath, heather-clad with scrub bushes, many stones, gorse and numerous clumps of pines. The land near to Blackbushe Airport is similar to this today. It also had quite a number of steep little hills, and in the Collingwood Park areas there were still some of the trees that James Laurell had planted way back in the early 1800's, on his Fir Plantation.

Much of the land required for the course was owned by two people, Mr J.F.Wright of Frimley Hall, and Mr Temple-Cooke who lived at "Edmonscote". West of Prior Road the other land required for the course was owned by Mr Gooch, who had recently died, and smaller portions belonged to General O'Grady Haley's widow, of "Whitegates", and to two other house-owners bordering the course. East of Prior Road all the land required belonged to Mr Wright, Mr Flaxman of "Beaufront" and "Hillcrest", and the Royal Albert Orphanage. A smaller portion on either side of Prior Road belonged to the Goldney family.

In the grounds of Frimley Hall, Mr Wright, who was a keen golfer, had constructed a small pitch and putt course, to which he no doubt invited some of his friends and neighbours to play, and so it is not surprising that the first preliminary meeting to investigate the possibility of building a full 18 hole course in Camberley was held at Frimley Hall. Camberley already had a small, rather wet 9 hole course at that time, sited on Barossa Farm, but that was all.

Mr Wright and Mr Temple-Cooke called this meeting of their friends, together with other residents living in the Portsmouth and Chobham Roads, early in 1912. It was then decided to set up a small sub-committee charged with the task of approaching the owners of the land required for the course to ascertain from them their terms for either selling or leasing their land to the new club, and to obtain their willingness to co-operate in the venture. In addition to Mr Wright and Mr Temple-Cooke, Mr Hollings of "Watchetts House", Mr Brenton of "Ravenswood" and Captain Harris of "The Cairnies", the sub-committee had Mr E.T.Close, a solicitor, and Mr Northcott, a bank manager, as additional members, with Mr Close acting as Hon.Secretary.

Enquiries with landowners commenced, and on May 14th when the sub-committee met again it transpired that 7 of the required landowners had agreed to sell their land and the other 4 to lease theirs.

The sub-committee then estimated that the initial sum required to start the project off was some £8,000, of which £1,000 would be required for the Club House. The Club was also to have some tennis courts and a croquet lawn. They were of the opinion that the best way to raise this sum was to form a Golf Club Company, and to issue Debenture shares of either £300 or £100. The Hon.Secretary said that he had already been promised £7,500 towards this sum from a number of people if the Company was formed.

A fortnight later the full committee of 30 prospective members met. It was formally agreed to proceed with the formation of a Club and Golf Course

Company, and a board of 5 Directors of the Company appointed, charged with the task of finding the finance for the project and constructing the course. The Debentures to be issued were to carry certain playing rights to those who bought them, and these were destined to change hands many times since they were originally sold.

It appears that no provision was made in the Articles of Constitution of the Company to enable the club members as a whole to purchase back these Debentures from the few individuals who owned them at a set price on a specific date in the future, so that the Club members would then own their own course rather than play golf on land owned by a Company from whom they did not even have a lease of any sort. Stranger still is the fact that, despite this anomally and the non-existence of any lease, this arrangement worked so well over the first 75 years of the Club's existence. Of course the arrangements were first made in a period when it did not occur to the gentlemen who first bought the Debentures that any commercial instincts might ever intrude, or land values inflate so much. They were all golfers themselves, they still are today, and just so long as this state of affairs continues and the Company and the Club members both have the same objective in mind, that of preserving Camberley Heath Golf Course as an enjoyable amenity for its fortunate members and its preservation as an essential "open breathing space" amidst what is now a densely populated residential area, so all will be well. This is what really matters in any discussion about the Club's future!

Back to 1912! By August 3rd Mr Colt had been appointed as architect of the course by the Directors and Mr Franks put in charge of its construction. A "Building Committee" for the Club House was set up, and Mr H.R.Poulter appointed as the architect. Many of the large houses in Collingwood Park and on the Waverley Estate were designed by him, his "trademark" invariably being a small round tower with a little conical roof appearing on the corners of these houses. The Club House has this feature, and it can also be seen on a shop on the corner of High Street and Princess Way, and on a house in Parkway named "Trevince". Tenders were invited for building the Club House, and eventually one of £3,957 from Messrs. Kemp accepted. Meanwhile quotations for a supply of water to the course were under way and the road connecting the Club House to Portmouth Road was being made. A Mr Toogood was appointed as Head Groundsman, and he was also to become the Club's professional upon completion of the course's construction at a salary of £2 a week. (Multiply by about 60 to get a comparable salary in 1987).

By May 1913 a General Committee was formed to allow the election of members to proceed and some 220 members joined. Although the course was not yet completed some play commenced, and as the Club House, which had been designed as a Dormy House so that members who wished to do so could stay there for a few days, approached completion, its domestic staff was engaged. This consisted of a steward and his wife, a cook, housemaids, kitchenmaids and waiters, some of whom were to "live in" the Club House. The salaries to be paid were agreed by the committee members, who themselves owned the big houses nearby and thus would be paying their own staff on a comparable basis. These are worth quoting as an insight into this period. They were:

Cook	£40 a year and all found.
Housemaid	£25 a year and all found.
Kitchenmaid	£16-18 a year and all found.

Caps and aprons for waitresses to be supplied.
Steward and his wife £60-80 a year and all found.

As most of the owners of large houses all employed some 5-10 servants themselves, this gives some idea of their own staff wage bills, remembering one must multiply by about 60 to compare with 1985.

Captain Warren Hastings was appointed as the Club Secretary, and on January 1st 1914 Prince Albert of Schlesswig Holstein officially opened the course by driving off the first tee.

Another sidelight on this period was a Committee meeting minute authorising the club to supply the regular caddies with a pair of boots! Transport of members to and from the club was also arranged by the committee. Few members had motor cars, and most who did not live near to the course came by train to Camberley station, and some who lived nearby came by bicycle. So the club arranged with Messrs Drake and Mount to run a horse bus from the station to the course twice a day; a motor signboard and white posts were erected on Golf Drive to point the way to the Club House; and a lean-to bicycle shed was put up. The horse bus fare was 6d each way, but later on the cab proprietors charged 2/6 owing to the hilly nature of the route. In the Club House a 3-course hot lunch cost 2/-, a cold lunch 1/6, and, if you were staying in the Dormy House, a fire in your bedroom cost 1/6.

In 1914, Lord Saltoun gave a cup for a Scratch competition, and Mr Wright one for a Handicap Knockout competition. Sad to say, Lord Saltoun's son, Lieutenant Simon Fraser was killed just after the war broke out, and Mr Wright's son, who had served throughout the war after leaving Sandhurst, died in the influenza epidemic of 1919.

Mr Toogood's services were not considered satisfactory, and he was replaced by Mr P.Gaudin as the club professional, and he played an exhibition match with Harry Vardon, Ted Ray and J.H.Taylor soon after the course opened, and just before World War I commenced.

During World War I, officers training in the locality were offered temporary membership at much reduced rates, and great efforts were made to keep the Club House going by trying to attract people to stay there for considerable periods at special rates.

The Secretary, Captain Hastings, was called up and two members of Germanic birth resigned, although they had lived in England for many years. In 1915 girl caddies were employed! In 1915 Gaudin resigned as professional to take up an appointment in America, and was replaced by Pennington. Great efforts were made to keep the course going, and Mr Waterer of the Bagshot nurseries, who was a member, consented to act as foreman of the groundsmen. The Debenture holders were asked to forego the 4% interest on their shares, and I think it quite probable that they have never taken the interest due to them at any time since. In 1917 the Club advertised for women to work on the course owing to the shortage of men, and the lady members complained to the committee that they had to go through the men's locker room to get to their bathroom. However, whisky was 1/- a tot! Such was life in the Golf Club at the end of the quite terrible 1914-18 war.

The membership right up to the 1930's was mainly of an aristocratic nature, with a predominance of men with a military or high professional background. The Golf Club was indeed the focal point of "Camberley Society's" club-life. It was not until the year 1946 that anyone from "trade" in the town was accepted for membership, when one or two, amongst whom was my father, were elected.

Just recently the Club, which has flourished so happily for so many years, has been put on the open market by the Company's Directors to the consternation of its members and all the surrounding residents who fear that a change of ownership might in some way impair the amenity everyone so enjoys through the existence of this course.

Camberley Heath Clubhouse and the 18th fairway. Built in 1913, it epitomises the era of which it was such a notable part, the meeting place of Camberley's "Landed Gentry".

View from the 5th tee illustrates how the course was cut out from the Fir Plantation made by James Laurell in Cart Bottom.

CHAPTER 19

World War I created great changes in Britain and the British Empire and, although these were not very apparent at first, by the time we became embroiled in yet another World War in 1939 it became only too obvious that the end of our great Empire was in sight.

These "between the wars" changes were accompanied by slow but very real changes in the social structure of our country. The rise in status and in the "life-style" expectations of the middle and working classes of our people nationwide was reflected, to some extent, in Camberley as elsewhere.

The General Strike of 1926 was the first post-war flexing of Trade Union Power. It started on May 1st, whereupon the Government declared a State of Emergency and took steps to control food supplies, commandeer all forms of transport and preserve order. Amateur drivers etc. volunteered to keep things going and the strike only lasted 9 days before it was called off.

I have said before that Camberley was a Military University town, and this was indeed so, right up until 1940, when Industry started to arrive here. In fact the very first industrial firms arrived just after the start of World War II, but these only operated on a very small scale in Bridge Road and Doman Road, which had just been developed. This meant that from 1918 until 1939 there were practically no other opportunities for employment in any other sphere than that of attending to the needs of the R.M.C. and the Staff College and the landed gentry who lived here. True, the increased mobility of everyone improved with the rapid development of the motor car and the railway and omnibus services, allowing some of our townsfolk to seek employment away from Camberley, and this also had some influence upon the growth of our residential area.

The Royal Aircraft Establishment had been set up at Farnborough just before the end of World War I, and another large military camp at Deepcut about 1900, and this enabled a few small firms to exist here making parts required for the aircraft industry. The London Road (A30) now became an increasingly busy thoroughfare, thus bringing employment to the garages, inns and restaurants that sprang up alongside it. The railway service to London had two trains running every hour and took $1\frac{1}{4}$ hours of travelling time, thus enabling some Camberley residents to commute to work there each day.

As Camberley's population slowly increased from 13,500 in 1918 to about 19,000 in 1939 there was a little more employment open to the middle and working classes in retail and service shops. By 1930 we had four ladies' hairdressing salons in the town. Electricity came to Camberley in 1922, and we had a telephone service which dated back to the turn of the century.

In 1939 the interior of the trading area enclosed by Park Street, London Road, the High Street and the railway (comprising the area we now call the Town Centre) was occupied by two small schools, one a Council School and the other a voluntary Church School, both of which had paved school playgrounds. Park Street, Obelisk Street and Princess Street were still lined with the rows of semi-detached cottages, each with a small garden, that had been built there by Captain Knight in Victorian times, some of which were let to the domestic servants and the gardeners working in the large houses of the landed gentry. The commercial section of the 1935 Camberley Street

Directory listed 22 gardeners as being in full time employment in these, and quite a few of them were housed in cottages on the estates in which they worked.

The war years of 1914-1918 brought tragedy to quite a few of Camberley's great houses. Our War Memorial carries the names of the sons as well as the owners of many of these. Those who lost their sons were Squire Hollings of the "Watchetts", Alderman A.C.Pain of "St.Catherines", Dr Cadell of "Elmhurst", Dr Scott of "Tudor Lodge", Mrs Mackenzie of "Collingwood Grange", Lady Pennington of "Heathstock", Mr Fowler of "Old Dean Hall" and Lady Elphinstone of "Pinewood", Bagshot. Among the estate owners were Brigadier-General Findlay and Lt.Colonel Furse both of "Alphington", Brigadier-General Currie of "Minley Manor", and Colonel Boileau of "Elstowe", all killed, as well as many of our townsfolk, of whom Ken Clarke has written in his book of "Camberley at War" in the tragic slaughterhouse of World War I.

In the case of Squire Hollings in particular, the loss of his son and heir was to make a considerable difference to Camberley's industrial and residential development. Upon his death in 1922, his daughter Hildegarde, who was married to a naval officer, Lt. Commander Venn, inherited the Watchetts and Bristow Farm estates, which she sold to Mr Nicholas Verran in 1924. The Verran family had come to Camberley about 1897 from Truro in Cornwall, and had established a very flourishing butchers and fishmongers business in the London Road near to its junction with the High Street. At the rear of the premises was their abattoir, the road to which was the service road that is now at the side of Allders Store in Obelisk Way. As a child, I well remember seeing the cattle and pigs being driven up this road to the slaughterhouse, and the horrible noises that came from there afterwards. The Verran family prospered, for they certainly knew their business, and I can truthfully say that I think they were the best butchers Camberley has ever had. Mr Nicholas Verran had a large house in Knoll Road called "Tresamble", situated where the Charles Church offices are now, and he invested very wisely in Camberley's future by purchasing the Watchetts and Bristow Farm estates. In 1929 he put the farm and a portion of the Watchetts (Parkway and Watchetts Drive) up for auction. 120 housing plots of about 1/3 acre, with frontages of 40 feet, were offered in the Watchetts, but with a restrictive clause in the conveyance precluding any purchaser from building anything other than a two storied house which, without including the land purchase price, had to cost a minimum of £630 (probably about £65,000 at 1980 prices); this to ensure that all houses on the estate would not fall below a certain standard. This was the second effective effort made by an estate developer in Camberley at what is today called "Area Town Planning": ie. placing together houses that those of a certain "income-group" will occupy. The houses on the Watchetts Estate were almost the first 3 and 4 bed-roomed houses built predominantly for the middle classes then emerging in Camberley.

The fields of Hacklane Farm that were enclosed between Watchetts Drive, Parkway, Park Road and Frimley Road, behind the new houses, were acquired by the F.& C.U.D.C. to enable them to construct the Watchetts Recreation Ground and Camberley Grammar School, now a Middle School, with its playing fields.

Watchetts House with its two lakes and its surrounding pleasure grounds was sold to Mr R.Over. A few houses were built on the south side of Watchetts Drive, but the rest of these ex-Hacklane Farm fields continued to be farmed by Mr King on lease. Eventually they were sold in the 1960's to the Surrey Education authority for France Hill Secondary School to be built there with its playing fields surrounding it. This school, which had up till that date been housed in old Franzhill House, had by that time grown so big that what is now the Adult Education Centre could no longer contain it, and it had to move elsewhere.

Some 30 houses on 30 foot frontages were built in Crabtree Road, which was a very old road track leading to Bristow Farm, but in 1938 Bristow Farm itself, together with 133 acres of farmland, was sold to Mr J.James, except for a portion of ground in the extreme north of the farm where it abutts the Peat Moor. This had been bought by the F.U.D.C. for them to construct a Sewage Works which is still there. Mr Job James had previously been the owner of Rosemary Farm in Blackwater, and he promptly sold Bristow (via Mr Kinlock, a merchant banker) to the Surrey Border and Camberley Railway Company. At that time Bristow Farm comprised a series of meadows with two large but separate copses, known as Watchetts Wood and Cove Wood, situated amidst them.

A miniature narrow gauge railway track was constructed along the Blackwater River valley joining Cove Wood near Frimley, to Vale Road by the Peat Moor. It was just a pleasure railway with small carriages, constructed mainly to delight children with a ride through fields that in springtime abounded with wild flowers. Unfortunately for the railway company, World War II broke out just 18 months after the railway started up, and in November 1939 the company went into bankruptcy; a Receiver was appointed, and the F.& C.U.D.C. purchased the land a year later. (Photograph, Page 82)

Bristow Farmhouse itself, which still exists in Westfield Road on the "James Road Estate" was bought by Mr Percy White (of Whites Garage). It has now been divided into 3 parts, and its small garden is entirely surrounded by houses.

Little did the previous owners of the rather ordinary, often water-logged fields and copses of Bristow Farm and neighbouring Park Farm realise that one day this land would become Camberley's Industrial Area and the land attain a considerable value in consequence.

A service at our War Memorial outside the gates of the Staff College in 1935. The whole town stopped for the 2 minute silence on Armistice Day right up until about 1950.

CHAPTER 20

The 10 year period that followed World War I saw the development of the Tekells Castle and Pine Woods estates.

That part of the original Tekells Castle Estate which had been retained by General Byrne after he had disposed of the Brackendale, Waverley and Pine Woods estates, had been sold to Mr A.Wilson-Hughes four years after the General's death in 1898.

After his acquisition of the Castle in 1902 he spent some £4,000 in the erection of a new wing and re-modelling the interior of the older part, and also added four tennis courts and a croquet lawn to the gardens.

In 1905 he put the estate on the market but no buyer was found. At mid-day on a Friday in October 1906 he left the Castle, which was then fully and beautifully furnished, to go to Salisbury. Whilst he was away a fire occurred whose origin was thought to be a complete mystery. One theory was that there had been a gas explosion causing a large hole to appear in the Castle's wall. Apparently Mr Wilson-Hughes had left three gas jets burning when he left the house to give the appearance of the house being occupied at night time, and possibly this might have caused the fire. At the time of the fire it was understood that Mr Wilson-Hughes had not fully insured himself against his loss, and would be a considerable loser over the catastrophe. Even so, apparently he had some difficulty in extracting the insurance money from his insurers! Tekells Castle has long since disappeared. It was situated on the uppermost of the three terraces that lie some 50 yards to the right of the Tekels Park Guest House, which has been built on the site of a part of the old stable block.

In the late 1920's housing development commenced on a small portion of the Tekells Castle Estate. The plan of the estate showed the construction of a proposed new road connecting Park Road to the Tekells Estate. The first part of this, which would run alongside the already made Brackendale Road, would be through Captain Knight's old Kingsclear/Heathcote House estate, but upon reaching the Tekells Estate it would bend first east and then south around the site of the old Castle. The whole of this proposed road had in fact been one of the original driveways from Cambridge Town to Tekells Park in Captain Knight's day, and was to be called Tekells Avenue.

By 1939 some 20 plots of between 1-3 acres had eventually been built upon in the Tekells Park Estate and 10 more houses built in the first part of Tekells Avenue on the eastern "Heathcote House" side of the road. These latter were the first houses there and their occupants are still accorded the rights of access to what is now the private Tekells Park, probably in continuance of the clause inserted in the Tekells Castle Estate sale notice of 1870 by Captain Knight which stated that the occupants of "Heathcote House" were always to have access to the Tekells Estate.

Tekells Park is a lovely place and its preservation as an open space is, in my opinion, of great importance to Camberley together with Camberley Heath Golf Course and the few Recreation Grounds we have. To this one might tentatively add the old Royal Albert Orphanage grounds, but the fate of this area is at the moment a matter of considerable speculation.

In 1929 Tekells Park was bought for the Theosophical Society with funds from the Liberal Catholic Church in Holland. The grounds were put back in order and a lecture hall and several houses then built, one of which, built in Dutch Colonial style, borders the meadows that are part of the Park. There is another house built in this style in Springfield Road - I wonder if there is any connection between these two houses?

For those of my readers who may not know of this, the Theosophical Society was founded in the U.S.A. in 1875. My encyclopedia states this as their objective, "The system aims at establishing a universal brotherhood by showing the unity of all religions, especially in their esoteric teaching, manifested by occult phenomena".

The Guest House provides facilities for Seminars of their Society and is also available to other groups. They have two halls and a separate study room, as well as a number of rooms in which visitors may stay. There is a very nice restaurant in which vegetarian food is served, and this is open to non-residents. The gardens surrounding it all go to make this a very pleasant and peaceful place, just as it must have been in the past and, one hopes, will continue to be in the future years ahead of us.

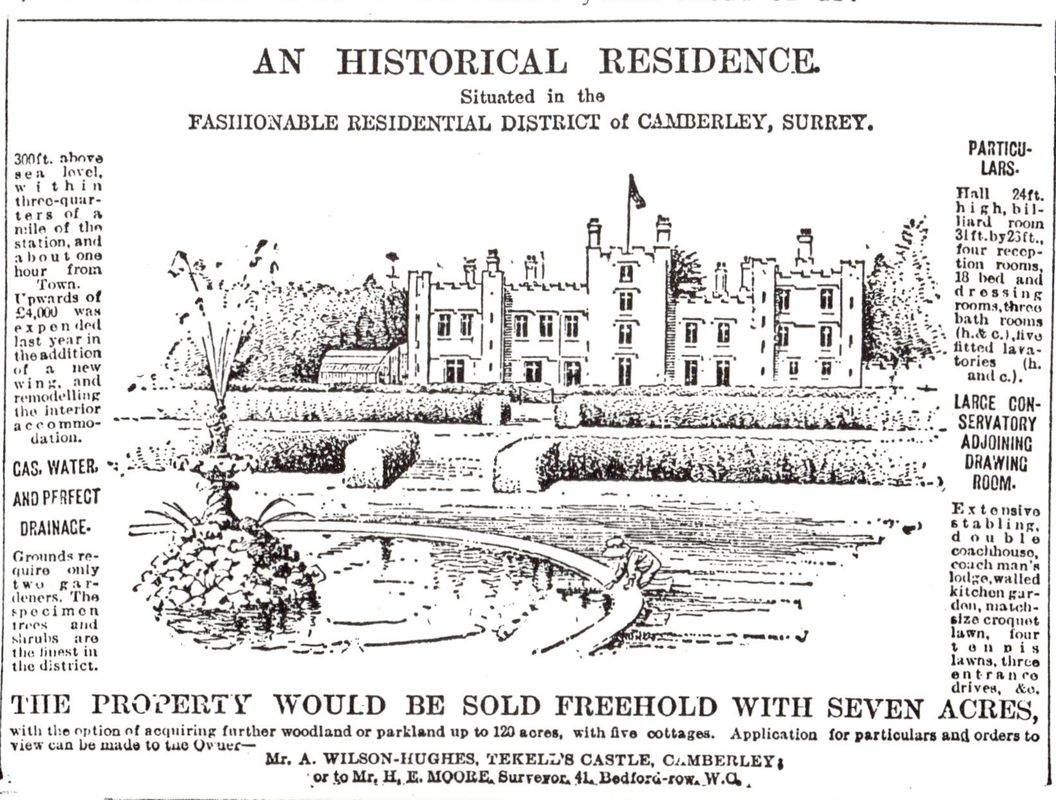

Above: The sale notice of Tekells Castle in 1905. The new wing added by Mr Wilson-Hughes is on the right of the building.

Below: The Tekels Park Guest House built on the site of the old Stable Block and the Coachmans House.

CHAPTER 21

The period "between the wars" also saw the development of part of the Pine Woods Estate. Grange Road and Belton Road, forming a loop, had been constructed just before World War I and two or three houses built there. By 1939 another ten houses had been built bordering those roads and adjoining this, on the Waverley Estate, Grove Road had been made and five houses with very large gardens now surrounded this cul-de-sac. The most beautiful part of the Pine Woods Estate, Walkers Ridge, was not constructed until after World War II. This runs along one of the "toes" of Crawley Hill which is shaped just like the map of Italy. From here there are really lovely views looking down over Tekells Park towards Frimley, the lights of which twinkle below at night time, and also those of Heatherside away to the left.

Alongside the Chobham Road and bordering the 15th and 16th fairways of Camberley Heath twelve houses were built, several of which had two or three acres of ground. This strip of land had once been part of the "Edmonscote" and "Gooch" estates. Just south of Chobham Road, land from the "Edmonscote" (now called "Frimley Place") estate had been sold for "Carwarden House" to be built for Sir John Carden. This is now the Teachers Training Centre. Three other houses, one of which was "Winding Wood", were built nearby. Lord Guy Alvingham, a guards officer, lived there in the 1950's. The houses by the golf course were, as one might expect, lived in by keen golfers. One of these was "Larkswood", which had a heather garden in front which was a riot of lovely colours in August, and was the home of the Chetwood family. Another was "The Rough", in which Brigadier Jelf lived - he too was a keen golfer.

On the bordering Heatherside Estate, which for very many years only had five houses on it, "Prior Place", "Heatherside House", "Yockley", "Edgemoor" and "Heatherside Farmhouse", two more were added - "Millbrook House", now the home of Mr Ken Bond, and a beautiful old house "Old Knowles", both of which are still there.

In March 1921 the first Council house was built in Camberley by the F. & C.U.D.C. on the Barossa Housing Estate.

Towards the end of World War I the Ministry of Health had called upon all local councils to estimate the number of working class houses needed and in Camberley this had led to the formation of the "Houses for Working Class" committee, and the decision to build thirty four semi-detached houses at Barossa at a cost of £885 each, and also sixteen at Frimley Green. Most of the houses contained a parlour, a 16' x 11' living room, a scullery, larder, bathroom and three bedrooms. Judged by the standards of Council houses built elsewhere in Britain, these were of very good quality. The Barossa Estate was our Council's first venture in this respect to be followed by many more in the years to come.

At that period in our town's development there was only a comparatively small requirement for this type of house in Camberley. Captain Knight's rows of cottages in the Park Street area, and the small houses around the Frimley Road, Vale Road area, had hitherto provided sufficient accommodation of this type, remembering our population was only 13,500 in 1920. Further demand for Council house developments did not become apparent until shortly before World War II when our population reached 19,000, and the James Road Council house estate was commenced, starting from Crabtree Road on Bristow Farm.

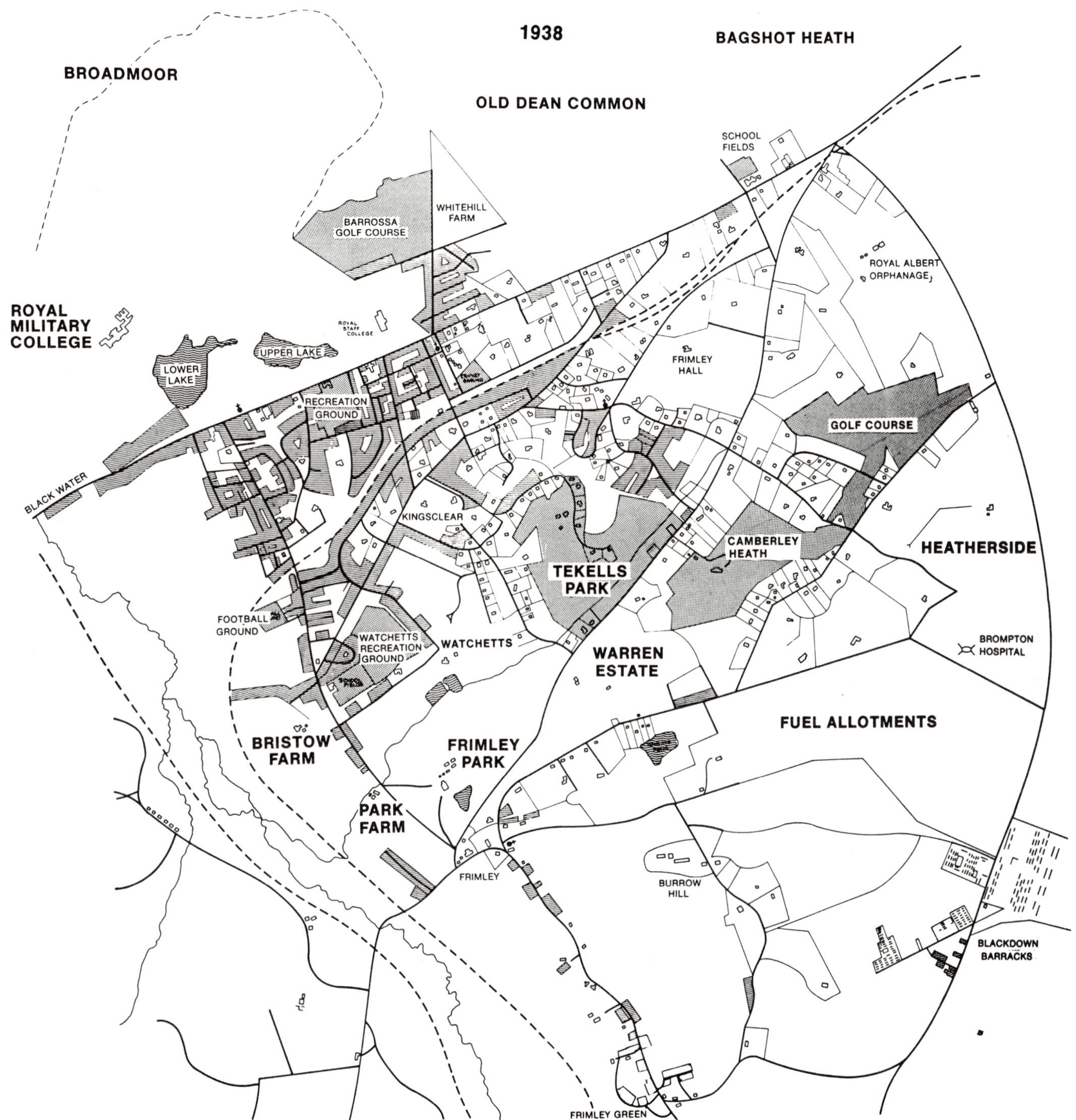

<u>Population:</u>

1938 - 19,000 est.

Between the end of WW1 in 1918 and the start of WW2 in 1939 there had been little change in the residential area of Camberley. Development commenced on the Watchetts Estate in 1930 and on the Tekells Estate, which had been sold to the Theosophists Society in 1920, and some houses were also built around Camberley Heath Golf Course. Franzehill Park, now called the France Hill Estate continued it's expansion. Council housing was erected on Barossa and on Bristow Farm. The six farms that lay between Frimley and Frimley Green that had once belonged to the Lord of Frimley Manor were still intact but the Warren Farm had a small development of Council houses opposite to where there had once been a Workhouse.

In 1939 the main shopping area of Camberley was almost entirely confined to the High Street, with just a sprinkling of shops in the London Road and Park Street. Both sides of the High Street had by now been fully developed, with 90 shops located there. London Road still had only a thin line of shops stretching from the High Street corner to Park Street, amongst which was the Post Office (where the T.S. Bank is) and the Camberley & District Club, a few near the Municipal Offices, and then another thin line in Yorktown. In Park Street there was one cluster of shops, consisting of a butcher, baker, dairyman and fishmonger opposite Obelisk Street and, near to Princess Street, Mr Williams had his ironmongers shop with a tobacconist close by. Apart from these and the two Inns that had been there since 1860, the rest of Park Street only had a garage and several rows of cottages.

One of the High Street shops belonged to Frederick Robinson, a photographer especially renowned for his portraiture of children. Marcus Adams of London and "Freddy" were the two foremost artists in the country famed for this particular form of their art, and Mr Robinson was elected the National President of the Royal Photographic Society about 1950, the highest honour in his profession that he could receive. His studio was situated where Camberley Stationers is now, and his sister, Elsie who, amongst many other skills, was a highly talented amateur cabinet-maker, started a gift shop there in the front part of his studio. This was the place to go for anyone who wanted something very special at Christmas time, for birthdays or to mark a family celebration. Elsie had exquisite taste in the choice of goods that she bought to sell in her shop. She was an outstanding window-dresser and the centre piece of her displays was often a very beautiful flower arrangement. She always had a plentiful supply of rare and lovely plants from which she was able to choose for these arrangements, as her brother was the owner of a wonderful garden. This was at "Snaprails", a large house in Sandhurst, in which his whole family resided. The garden had a stream running through it, and the whole place was an absolute riot of colour throughout the summer with many lovely azaleas and rhododendrons. He and Elsie did most of the work in this huge garden themselves, getting up early in the morning to do so. Once a year it was opened to the public, and the many people who went there enjoyed what was in reality a delightful garden party. "Snaprails" has now become a public park maintained by Sandhurst Parish Council, and houses have been built on much of the garden it once had.

By 1939 the High Street had altered very considerably from its pre-World War I character. Long gone were the days when at the start of each term at the R.M.C. the "Cadet Races" used to take place. Before there were many motor cars, almost every cadet used to arrive at Camberley station at the same time on the same train. A fleet of horse-drawn cabs awaited them and there was great rivalry to secure a cab. From then on, a hotly contested race ensued to be the first one to get through the town and the College gates, and arrive at the Old Building. When I was very young, I recollect an occasion when these spirited young men removed the horse from between the shafts of one of the cabs, and replaced it with a team of some 20 of them. With great joy, this was then run through the High Street and London Road with one young gentleman as its "cabby" driver sitting on the box with his luggage. I was told that after this, both he and the cab finished up in the Lower Lake. Quite a celebration! Maybe to mark the end of horse-cabs and the take over by the motor cabs in Camberley!

Another notable occasion occurred at the end of World War I when the cadets hung an effigy of the Kaiser from the telephone wires in the London Road and then burnt it.

The Victory Parade in Camberley High Street in 1918. The Station is in the background. "Freddy Robinson's" old shop, now Camberley Stationers, is just out of the picture to the right.

Getting ready for the "Cadet Races". Cabbies lined up waiting for the Cadets to arrive off the train and then start the dash to be first at the Old Building in the R.M.C.

By the time World War II commenced, we had two schools in Knoll Road - the "Crammer" for young would-be cadets at "Holmdale", and next to this "The Knoll", a very select boarding school for some 30-40 young ladies, aged 8 to 17. No doubt, the close proximity of these two schools led to high jinks at times. In addition to Miss Crisp's Preparatory School for Boys and Girls, Mrs Mortimer had started a School for Dancing, which was to become the famous Elmhurst Ballet School after the War. Meanwhile, three other private Preparatory Schools had started. One was at Cordwalles on the London Road, and the others were Cheswycks in Firwood Drive and Lyndhurst in Woodlands Road. Beaufront, the boarding school for girls established at the turn of the century in the Portsmouth Road, was still going strong, also the three primary schools mentioned in Chapter 30, and Camberley Grammar School. Cordwalles is now incorporated into a State School, and The Knoll boarding school is no longer there, but the others have all survived to the present day, though some are in different locations.

In 1987 we have a proliferation of Women's Clubs, but in 1939 Camberley had only a few. These were mostly in connection with one or other of the churches, or in support of a charity. However, we did have a Girls Friendly Society, a Girls Fellowship Club and Girl Guides, and there were several Womens Institutes for more elderly ladies. Also, there was a Choral Society and an Operatic Society with a membership composed of both men and women. The men were rather better catered for. They had the Working Mens Club as well as the District Club for "beer and billiards"; several Masonic Lodges for the Initiates; and the British Legion for old war-time comrades and their friends. Then there were Football and Rugby Clubs, cricket and golf, bowls and tennis for all those who enjoyed sport.

For the young business executives, the Round Table Club had been formed in 1935, though a Rotary Club was not started until 10 years later, with a very jolly parson, the Rev. Stephens of the Congregational Church, as its first President. For those who were seriously minded and liked to listen to highly informative lectures and talks on a large variety of subjects, there was the Camberley Brotherhood, who met once a month. But this organisation ceased during the War and was not re-started afterwards, as was the Round Table.

Today the Camberley News lists well over a hundred different Clubs and Societies who meet regularly in the town, together with the names of the organisers one should contact with a view to joining. They offer an infinite variety and range of interests and at last, yes at last! - we even have an indoor swimming pool in our new Arena Leisure Centre.

A street party in Harcourt Road, Yorktown to celebrate the end of World War II

CHAPTER 22

World War II commenced on September 1st, 1939. The run-up to this had started in 1935 when Hitler came to power in Germany and ordered conscription. A Camberley News report at that time of a speech by our own M.P. for the Farnham division, Sir Arthur Samuel, shows that he for one had clearly seen the eventual consequences of this, and Hitler's determination to break every treaty that had been made with Germany. Over the next four years, Germany under Hitler first remilitarised the Rhineland, then annexed Austria by force, separated the Sudetenland from Czecho-Slovakia followed by the annexation of Czecho-Slovakia itself in 1939 and Memel in Lithuania. He then made a pact with his arch enemy, Soviet Russia, on 23 August 1939, and followed this on 1 September by the annexation of Danzig in the Polish corridor and the invasion of Poland itself.

In 1937 Neville Chamberlain had become the British Prime Minister and, during these years, he pursued a policy of appeasement towards Germany and Italy (who had invaded Abyssinia) which led to the resignation of his Foreign Minister, Anthony Eden. In September of that year Chamberlain flew to Munich to meet Hitler, and a "piece of paper" was signed which reputedly was to avoid war. The travesty of this "Munich Agreement" was shown up within six months, when Hitler invaded Czecho-Slovakia. Only then did Britain wake up, and at last start to re-arm herself in earnest for the war that now seemed inevitable. Chamberlain tried to maintain peace by producing an alignment of European forces against Germany, but war inevitably came when Hitler invaded Poland, whose safety the consortium were pledged to defend, and war started for us on 3 September.

As Camberley was at that time predominantly a military town and many of its inhabitants had had years of service overseas, this came as no surprise to those living here. The Camberley News had carried their letters for some time, warning us to re-arm. Another topic near to the hearts of those who had served in India was the campaign afoot to achieve "Dominion Status for India". World War II was to be the means of achieving this for India and with it mark the start of the rapid break up of the British Empire and the end of the era that had been known as the "British Raj".

This era had known such great occasions as the Coronation Durbar, held in Delhi in 1911, when George V was crowned King of India, and the Prince of Wales' tour in 1922, when he strove to cement ties with India in the face of a Gandhi-inspired boycott.

Many of Camberley's "ex-patriot" community had lived through this era, an era in which the British residing abroad in the developing countries of Asia and Africa had held positions of great responsibility in these countries, with their word law in the many large isolated areas that they were called upon to administer almost single-handed. Granted that this was a situation that gave some of them rather inflated ideas of their own importance, which meant that they had considerable difficulty in coming to grips with the realities of life here upon their return to Britain. But it also instilled into the majority of them a great sense of duty towards the communities in which they lived, and when they retired here they carried on this sense of duty into their lives in Britain, to the undoubted advantage of their fellow townsmen. Many gave voluntary services to town councils, they organised charities, and their names were to be found on committees of all sorts.

In 1936 George V died, and his eldest son, the Prince of Wales, became Edward VIII, whose home was Fort Belvedere at Virginia Water, only to abdicate later that year and be succeeded by his brother, the Duke of York, as George VI. His daughter, Princess Elizabeth, who had done her A.T.S. training in Camberley during the war, came to live in Windlesham after her marriage to Prince Philip in 1947. I remember her visiting Camberley during that time when she opened the Exhibition of the Windlesham Camera Club, of which I was a member, and I thought how beautiful she was and how very gracious her short speech. She has visited Camberley several times since she became our Queen and has taken the salute at the Sovereign's Parade of the Royal Military Academy Sandhurst.

In these next chapters I will try to show what has happened to Camberley in the years that have followed the end of World War II. The transition of the Urban District of Camberley and Frimley which comprised Camberley, Frimley, Frimley Green, Deepcut and Mytchett, and had agriculture on the Blackwater farms and service to its military universities and landed gentry as almost its sole source of employment, to the Borough of Surrey Heath, which also includes Bagshot, Windlesham, Chobham, West End and Bisley, which is predominantly an industrial town with a military university in its midst, and where industry and the provision of services for those who work in industry provides at least 50% of the population with their means of livelihood, is the rest of my story.

The Prince of Wales visiting India in 1922

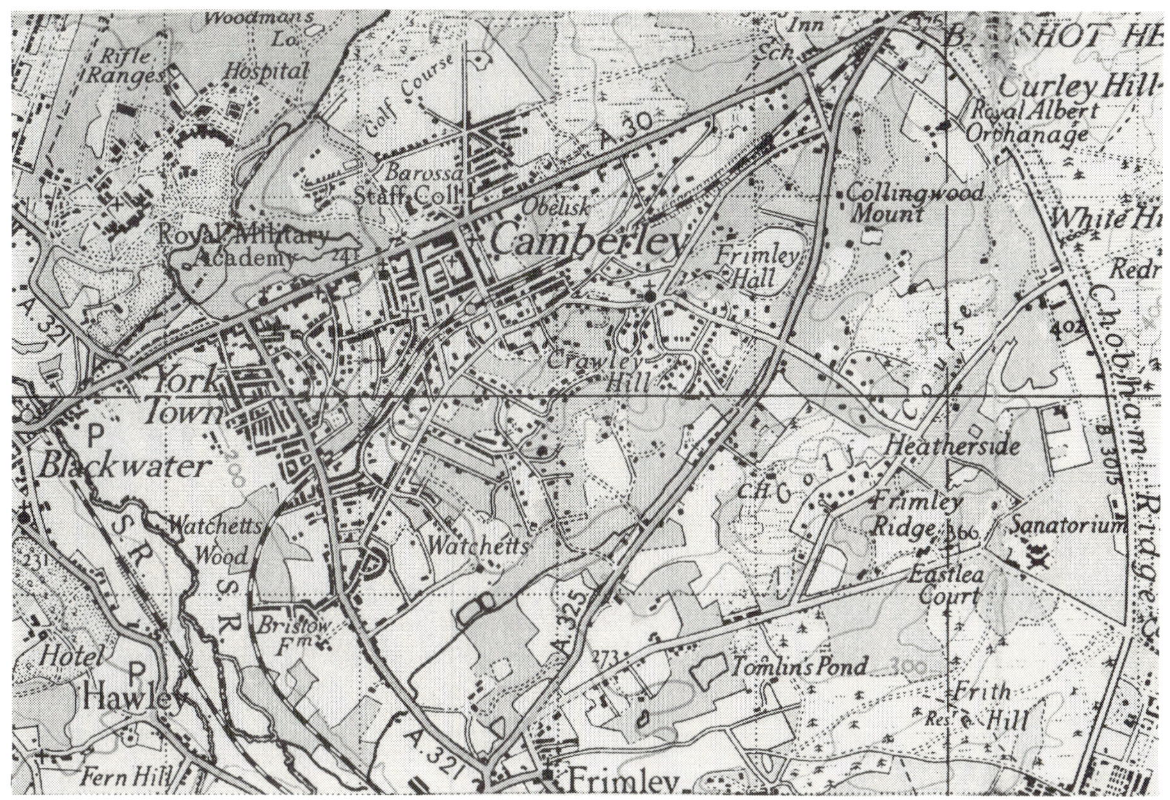

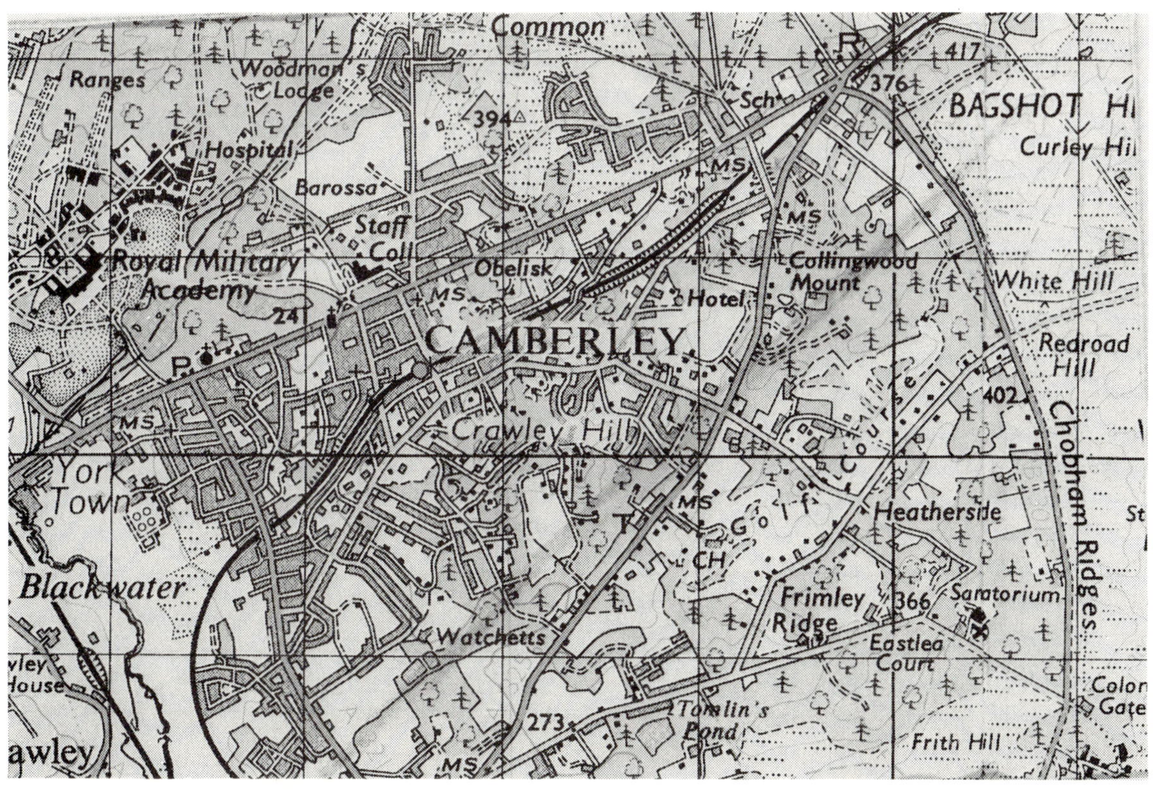

Comparison of 1939 Map above with 1959 Map below shows: Private Residential Developments; Warren Estate commenced; Watchetts Tekells, Waverley and Brackendale Estates $\frac{3}{4}$ built up; Road making being started on Collingwood Park Estate (Hillcrest Road); No development on Heatherside Estate; Army Staff Officers quarters on Barossa built; Council House building; James Road Estate $\frac{3}{4}$ completed; Old Dean Estate $\frac{1}{2}$ completed; Industrial Estate Development; Stanhope Road and Doman Road made and some factories appear on Yorktown Industrial Estate.

CHAPTER 23

The bombing of London and other large cities during World War II, with the destruction of their inner cores and the heavily populated areas within them, was a factor that undoubtedly motivated central government to commence a policy of dispersing the "overspill" inhabitants of large, crowded cities to surrounding country towns.

Starting in 1947, there was also a move to create "New Towns" by the colossal enlargement of what had hitherto been small towns or even villages. The first area to be developed in this way was at Harlow in Essex, soon to be followed by Stevenage to the north of London. The search then started for a site located in this area, much to the alarm of those who lived here and wished to conserve things as they were. What the "New Town" planners were looking for was a small town with huge areas of surrounding waste-land that they could obtain cheaply. To help them, the Government passed laws giving them sweeping powers of compulsory land purchase which terminated many of the rights of existing property owners in designated "New Town" development zones.

Needless to say, they looked at Camberley as a possible site for a "New Town", and in all probability it was only the firm hold of the Army upon their land to the north and east of Camberley and the existence of the Frimley Fuel Allotments to the south, that caused them to look elsewhere, and eventually to site their "New Towns" at Bracknell and Basingstoke. As an alternative to getting a "New Town" foisted on us, Camberley was required to house part of the "overspill" population of Carshalton, Mitcham, Esher, Surbiton, Sutton, Kingston, Wimbledon and Wallington, the eight Surrey towns forming the S.W. border of London. Either we could do this on a co-operative basis, which would allow us to control this population transfer, or lose control if it was done by compulsion. Fortunately for our town, our U.D.C. had some excellent Chairmen at that period. They had most unpalatable decisions to make during their terms of office, and it is largely owing to their strength of purpose in those difficult times that decisions were made by the U.D.C. which enabled Camberley to avoid being swallowed up by the "big city" and to retain its own individuality.

However, we had to take a large influx of new residents, none of whom came from a rural background, and this meant that efforts had to be made to attract industry here so that employment could be found for them. It also meant that new schools would be needed, hospitals would have to be enlarged, or new ones built, additional water, gas and electricity supplies found and sewage facilities constructed. Police forces would have to be augmented too.

But where was land to be found on which to build 1,250 new Council houses for these "overspill" residents? A programme of building by the U.D.C. to house our own existing residents had been started just before World War II on land purchased at Bristow Farm in the Crabtree Road area, and this had been pushed forward rapidly so that the James Road Estate was almost complete. Another Council estate was also under construction on Manor Farm east of the A321 road in Frimley, known as the Worsley Road Estate, (named after another excellent chairman of the U.D.C. Mrs Worsley). It was not possible to find room on either of these estates for the new "overspill" residents other than a very small number on the "Bain Avenue" extension of James Road. (Maps, Page 112 and Page 113.

This meant a search for entirely new sites. Four other farms lay between Frimley and Frimley Green, and the U.D.C. was able to purchase one of these of 41 acres, just north of the Worsley Road estate, and on this the Ansell Road estate was built. In Mytchett, on ground opposite to the "Miners Arms" Inn, there was a Greyhound Racing Track up for sale of 11 acres, and this enabled the "Rorkes Drift" estate to be enlarged. In the Chobham Road another small area of 11 acres to the rear of Heather cottages was also obtained. These estates, together with Bain Avenue, totalled 71½ acres, but a further 94 acres were still required.

There seemed to be only one place where this might be found - Old Dean Common - where in fact a 35 acre council estate to house some of our existing residents had already been started. This land had been purchased from the Crown, and in deference to local environmentalists' wishes, the estate had been set back some 75 yards from the A30 in order to preserve the delightful, wooded-look approach to Camberley from Bagshot along the London Road. Adjoining this estate was Cordwalles School with its playing fields, and a large house, "The Grove", that had at one time been the home of Sir Robert Watson-Smyth, both of which were built on the old Heathermount Estate.

To the rear of this, towards Saddleback Hill, open, pine-clad heathland stretched northwards for three miles to Caesars Camp near Easthampstead. The U.D.C. purchased 94 acres of this land to build a very large housing estate for our "overspill" residents, part of this sited on the ancient track that led from Gibbet Lane over the heath to Bracknell. Altogether the "overspill" population, many of whom came from the Wimbledon area, needed 165 acres to house them, and increased our population by 5,000 all within a space of 2 to 3 years. The arrangements that had to be made to accommodate these new residents undoubtedly commenced Camberley's post-war development.

The next problem facing our Council was how to find work for all these new people. Granted, that due to the loss of men killed in the War, combined with Britain's need to make good the damage done to our towns and replace ships and aircraft, we were in an era of so-called "full employment", but this had made little difference to us here.

Up until 1939 we had had no industry here, and by 1958, when the "overspill" started to arrive, we only had 32 fairly small industrial firms, all situated on the Yorktown Industrial Estate and in the surrounding streets. Practically all the employment available in these firms was already occupied by existing residents. Therefore it was essential that new industrial firms had to be encouraged to come here - but how was this to be done? And what sort of industry was there here already?

Assembling Oscillographs in Southern Instruments factory, 1958

CHAPTER 24

In the first ten years following World War II this was the employment situation in Camberley. The proximity of the Royal Aircraft Establishment at Farnborough had given rise to the location of a few small firms nearby who specialised in the up-and-coming electronic industry. Radar, which was in its infancy in Britain just before World War II, had been developed to a considerable degree by the time the war ended in 1945, and scientists were by then looking for peace-time uses of some of its components.

Two such scientists were Mr C.Brooke-Smith and Mr Colls, who founded a small firm employing 10 people, called "Southern Instruments", located at Fern Hill House in Hawley. Between them, they devised a number of uses for the oscillograph, some of which could be utilised for semi-automated factory processes. By 1952 their firm had grown to the extent that new and larger premises were needed, and the search for a suitable site commenced. It was winter time, but whilst driving along Frimley Road, Mr Brooke-Smith noticed that cattle grazing in the water-logged fields opposite to Frimley Park Manor House had sunk into the ground up to their knees but no further. From this he concluded that there must be a firm foundation here just below the surface, and that this area, of little use for farming, might very well be used for building factories. This proved to be the case, and he bought the land, built "Southern Instruments" here and so started up Camberley's second industrial estate at Park Farm.

Our first Industrial Estate had been established on the Peat Moor about 1950. F. & C.U.D.C. had purchased this site in 1949 from the Camberley Sand and Gravel Company and called it the Yorktown Industrial Estate. Soon afterwards, Doman Road and Stanhope Road had been constructed there, and development commenced.

During the war years, "Aeronautical Radio Services" and "Ancillary Developments" whose main concern was with the aircraft industry, had established themselves in Yorktown on the fringe of the Peat Moor in Doman Road and Surrey Avenue (off Vale Road). The former were Radio and Radar engineers, and the latter made Aeronautical navigation equipment. In Bridge Road, another firm "Aerolex" manufactured safety-harness seat belts for aircraft, and "Microcell", who made aircraft seating among other plastic products, had 6 divisions scattered in various localities in the nearby streets. "Eastmeads" in Frimley Road also made aircraft components as did "W.Myatts" in Stanhope Road.

That we had these firms was not only due to the R.A.E., but also to the close proximity of Blackbushe Airport. This had been constructed during the war as a Bomber Airfield because of its usually fog-free location on Hartford Bridge Flats. To assist aircraft to land in even the worst fog conditions it had a "Fido" light system installed, and the airfield was often used by aircraft from other locations who could not get back to their own aerodromes after bombing raids, because of the conditions there. After the war it was rapidly turned over to civilian usage, and Eagle Airways and Britannia Airways operated from there, some of the flights going to South Africa. As these Airway firms expanded, they outgrew Blackbushe and transferred to Gatwick, with the loss of some employment here, but fortunately by that time, some other firms not connected with the aircraft industry had come here.

One such was "Wilkinsons Linatex", who had first arrived in Camberley on Frimley Road in 1939 and who made rubber linings for industrial plant. Another firm was "All Wheel Drive", who manufactured earth moving equipment, tractors and snow-ploughs. They built two large factories on the new Stanhope Road, and their establishment marked the commencement of the Yorktown Industrial Estate's development. Soon other firms followed. Peppers of Woking, Gillone Electric, Lord's Controls, Rivlin Instruments, were all in the electrical, electronic or radio industries, as was Siba Electric, who became the second firm to establish themselves on Park Farm. Another large firm in the electronic industry, Solartron, started a factory at Farnborough nearby, and Sharples Centrifuges, manufacturing Marine Auxiliary Plant, also came to Camberley.

Employment for women was now being created on the new industrial estates both in their offices as well as on the factory floor. This was very welcome as, up until then, there had been little work for women available other than in shops and a few offices as an alternative to domestic service in the houses of the landed gentry. A new factory, the Yorktown Manufacturing Co, helped to improve this situation. They manufactured blouses and dresses for women and children, selling most of their products to Marks and Spencer, but some were sold in the town at "Arthur & Fred's" in the High Street. Another firm, Lorraine Knitwear, also helped to provide girls with work, as did Toni Cosmetics making home permanent waving kits in nearby Hawley Lane.

In 1947 "Athallan Grange", one of the homes of our landed gentry, fell prey to the industrial developer. This house, in Chobham Road, had at one time been the home of Mrs Spens, the lady who loved hunting but whose son had been killed on the Ash ranges. It was now bought by the Rheostatic Co who made thermostatic heating controls and this site is now occupied by the Marconi Co.

By 1958, thirteen years after the end of the war, 32 industrial firms had set up their factories in Camberley. Most of these were tucked away out of sight behind the houses in the Frimley Road, so that many of our residents did not even know that we had them there. This prompted the Camberley Rotary Club to stage a "Careers and Employment" Exhibition in 1958, held in the grounds of France Hill School, which at that time was in France Hill Drive. This was a great success, some 2,500 people attended it during the three days it was open, and it served a very useful purpose in acquainting Camberley people with the new avenues of employment that now existed here, some of which where hitherto unknown to many of them.

At that point in time, Camberley's "work" situation was perhaps the ideal one. We had just enough available for the number of people we had living here, and it was fairly diversified. But the situation we were about to face, when some 1,500 new "overspill" residents would be looking for jobs all within a space of a couple of years, would alter all this - so what was there here to attract new industrial employers to Camberley?

The first thing we had in our favour was that elsewhere in the country we were still in an era of "full employment" following the war years and the artificial boom that followed this, and so our somewhat unique situation of having a sudden surplus of labour in the district was an obvious attraction to employers thinking of opening a new factory.

Added to this was a second factor. This was the news that a new motorway, the M3, was to be constructed, joining Southampton and The Docks to London, and that this was to pass right through Camberley and, moreover, link up with other motorways, the M4 and the M25, on which construction had commenced. Easy access to the expanding motorway system was by this time becoming a number one priority to industrial firms for the transport of their products to their customers. Railway transport had become increasingly unpopular due to the uncertainty of delivery occasioned by strikes (amongst other factors), and road transport was taking its place, so that Camberley was well sited in this respect.

And lastly, industrial firms wanted to go where they were welcome, and could find decent living conditions for their employees. This was a matter for the District Council of any town to which they went, and in Camberley many found what they were seeking, with the result that our town today has a population of 55,000, most of whom are employed locally, and we are still growing!

Camberley Industrial Companies

NAME	ADDRESS	PRODUCTION
Aerolex Ltd.	Bridge Road	Aircraft components and equipment
All Wheel Drive Ltd.	Stanhope Road	Manufacturers and assembly of all wheel drive trucks, snow ploughs, and earth boring apparatus
Ancillary Developments	Surrey Avenue	Aeronautical Navigation Instruments
Aeronautical Radio Services	Doman Road	Radio and Radar Engineers
Denzil Skinner Ltd.	Portsmouth Road	Model Makers
Eastmead Engineering Co.	Frimley Road	Aircraft components and general engineering
S. & R. J. Everett & Co.	Victoria Avenue	Hypodermic Syringes
Gillone Electric Ltd.	Doman Road	Radio and T.V. components
H. Greenfield & Son	High Street	Manufacture ladies' outerwear
Inferation Ltd.	Stanhope Road	Heating Engineers
Janitor Boilers Ltd.	Vale Road	Domestic boilers
Lorraine Knitwear Co.	Park Street	Knitwear manufacture
Lord's Controls & A.C. Industries	Victoria Avenue	Electrical Control Equipment
W. Myatt Ltd.	Stanhope Road	Aircraft and light engineering
Microcell Ltd. :—		
Aircraft Engineering Div.	Stanhope Road	Aircraft parts and boats
Electronics Division	Blackwater	
Plastics Division	Bridge Road	Plastic laminates & mouldings
Artrite Resins Ltd.	Camberley	
Glass Yarns & Deeside Fabrics	Cromwell Road	Glass Fibre manufacture
Rubberishd Hair Division	10–14 Epworth St., London	
Peppers of Woking Ltd.	Stanhope Road	Electrical Engineers
Plastic Finishes Ltd.	Bridge Road	Plastics
Plextrude Ltd.	Murrels Lane	Plastics
Ramer Chemical Co.	Frimley Road	Synthetic Sponges
Rheostatic Co. Ltd.	Chobham Road	Thermostatic heating controls
Rivlin Instruments Ltd.	Doman Road	Electronic Instruments
Rainville Engineering Co.	Frimley Road	Light engineering, welding and cutting apparatus
Sharples Centrifuges Ltd.	Doman Road	Chemical, Process and Marine Auxiliary Plant
Salartron Electronic Group Ltd.	Farnborough	Electronic Engineers
Southern Instruments Ltd.	Frimley Road	Electronic measuring and recording equipment
Siba Electric Ltd.	Frimley Road	Automotive electrical equipment
Standard Insulators Ltd.	Bridge Road	Rubber grummets and rubber mouldings
Superstat Ltd.	Doman Road	Electronic Engineers
Toni Cosmetics	Hawley Lane	Home Permanent Waving Kits and Cosmetics
A. J. Watkins Ltd.	Doman Road	Engineers
Wilkinsons Rubber Linatex Ltd.	Stanhope Road	Rubber Engineers
Yorktown Manufacturing Co.	Doman Road	Manufacture of blouses and etc

1958 - A complete list of our Industrial Companies at that date.

CHAPTER 25

The industrial developments that occurred here between 1948 and 1958 gave an impetus to the demand for houses in Camberley, especially those for the expanding middle classes. Development of the Watchetts Estate, which had only just begun in the 30's, now continued along Park Avenue, Kingsley Avenue and Linkway, and some new houses were also built in the Diamond Hill/College Ride region. The Army, at last, decided to build some married quarters for the officers of the Staff College and R.M.A. and purchased Barossa Common from the Crown for this, at the same time that they bought Barossa Golf Course for their playing fields.

"The Warren" was the first of the great estates to be sold for housing development. Up until 1956 this 100 acre estate belonged to the three Connop sisters, and afterwards to their nephew, Colonel Newland. In 1958 the first houses were built in the southernmost part of the estate in Old Pasture Road, and the first part of Warren Rise leading off Chobham Road was soon built up. Further development occurred steadily over the next few years until the estate was completed. Sale of the houses was rapid and most were sold before completion.

But the great boom in housing, which was to make us the fastest growing town in Surrey, had not yet occurred. This was triggered off by the news that we were to have the M3 motorway constructed through a part of Camberley. The exact track that this was to take was the subject of public meetings, much discussion and considerable alarm from those who would be most closely affected by the noise that this new road would create. (Map, Page 113)

The result of all this controversy was to create a kind of hiatus in the housing developers' plans, until the route of the M3 was finally fixed. Going from west to east it would first divide the new industrial area into two parts: then travel through the southernmost parts of the Frimley Park, Watchetts and Tekells estates to Ravenswood Cross-Roads; and from here cut through Collingwood Park and divide the Royal Albert Orphanage estates into two. (The latter had become the W.R.A.C. College by then). Brackendale Road and Waverley Drive, which had previously allowed access to Camberley from the Portsmouth Road, were cut off, and all traffic from Frimley and the south-eastern part of Camberley could now only get to the Town Centre, across the M3, via Ravenswood Cross-Roads, Frimley Road or the Maultway.

Many older residents in Camberley thought that few people would want to live near the motorway because of the noise, but just how wrong that surmise has proved to be can be judged by the many housing developments that have since occurred bordering both sides of the road. Luckily for those living nearby, some three-quarters of the M3's route through Camberley is in a fairly deep cutting, and this has baffled the noise of the traffic to some extent, and much of the other part is raised above the houses and this has also helped to minimise its unpleasant effects.

Three other factors have added to the demand for new houses that has been almost constant here since 1960. The first of these has been the tight control that has been exercised by our Frimley and Camberley Urban District Council (now Surrey Heath Borough) over housing developments ever since the war and the consistency of their policy of "zoning" new residential areas by the density of housing they have allowed in different parts of the town.

In another form, that of "income-zoning", this was the policy started here as long ago as 1902, by Mr Thomas Boys, when he sold a part of Springfield Road on his Collingwood Park Estate with a stipulation that no house must be built there for less than £1,000, which was a great sum in those days. Mr Nicholas Verran carried on with this idea when he sold the first few plots of the Watchetts Estate in 1929, again with a clause in the conveyance of the land ensuring that all houses built there must cost more than £630, which sum produced houses worth £200,000 today. Long before Town Planning powers were invested in Local Councils, Camberley enjoyed a concerted policy in this respect, to the great advantage of us all today. It was our good fortune that so few landowners owned so much of the land here. They were far-sighted men and partly because it was in their own interests in preserving the value of as yet unsold land, and partly because they had no previous land-selling mistakes to rectify whereby land was depreciated through high-value and low-value houses having been built side by side, they were able to start from scratch and pursue consistent policies for the development of their estates.

There were two more factors which increased the demand for middle to higher income-group low density housing here. One was the proximity and rapid growth of Heathrow Airport, only 12 miles away, and the other the building of Bracknell New Town. We were just far enough away from Heathrow not to be bothered by the increasing noise from the many planes now arriving and departing from the Airport. But the crews of these planes wanted to get away from there in their off duty periods, and yet must not live too far away. Our new residential area was just right for them, and we have many air pilots living here today.

In Bracknell New Town, the outskirts of which stretch towards us as far as Caesars Camp on the other side of Old Dean Common, the professional planners did not really cater for the high income executives of Bracknell in their zoning policy, and they therefore looked around for accommodation further afield. Again, Camberley suited them very well, just as it had done the air pilots.

One other thing has helped to sell houses in Camberley. Right from the start, men about to retire have found it attractive. They still do. Leisure is not much use without someone to spend it with, and the many social and sporting activities available in clubs and organisations in Camberley provide both men and women with time to spare, outlets that provide both interest and companionship here today, just as they did 100 years ago.

The M3 Motorway under construction, 1969. Trees having been cleared, the Watchetts Stream is being piped into a culvert alongside the road.

CHAPTER 26

Central Area Re-development was taking place in many towns throughout Britain in the years that followed World War II. Some towns, such as Coventry and Plymouth, had had most of their shopping areas destroyed by bombing or fire and these areas provided the new "professors of town-planning" with heaven-sent opportunities to put their ideas into practice, starting from scratch and without having to adapt their plans in order to preserve existing buildings. Some towns had what the planners called "decaying centres": many others had become extremely congested with the growth of motor car travel and lacked adequate car parking facilities. Other towns were rapidly developing residentially and felt they had insufficient shops in their town centres to serve their projected population increase adequately.

In 1959 our Council deemed that such a situation existed here in Camberley. We had a fast growing population (25,000 then), insufficient car parks, and we only had shops in the High Street and the London Road, together with a few in Park Street. The rest of the area we now call the Town Centre comprised rows of small cottages built along Park Street, Princess Street and Obelisk Street about 1870, and a children's school that could be much better sited away from the shopping area. It was also thought that it would be good for trade in general in the town if we could persuade one or two of the big department stores to come to Camberley. Another project in mind, no doubt dear to the hearts of many Councillors, was a scheme to group all the projected civic buildings together on the eastern side of Knoll Road, (a plan just completed in 1986). The land required for this endeavour was the estate of a house called "Holmdale". Before World War II, this had been what was called a "Crammers School", a boarding school which existed to "cram" young, prospective, gentlemen cadets with enough knowledge to enable them to pass the entrance examination to the R.M.A. Sandhurst. It was then run by the Tinniswood family, and was quite an institution in Camberley, as was another specialist school that has since risen to national fame, Elmhurst Ballet School, originally started in far-off days as a Kindergarten for boys and girls.

By 1959, "Holmdale" had been acquired by the Council and its cricket ground, which they had purchased from "Hillside", turned into a car park for 150 cars. There was another car park holding 100 cars centrally situated for shoppers going to the High Street or London Road shops. This was in Obelisk Street, and on the site of what had once been the playground of another children's school.

In many respects we were still a village in those days, 75% of the shops were owned and run personally by their proprietors, and most shop keepers knew nearly all their customers by name. Courtesy and politeness were to be found in all shops, and indeed it could be taken for granted that one would get a pleasant reception wherever one went. The grocers and butchers ran delivery services to people's homes, and one could telephone an order to any of them. Mr Williams ran a real hardware shop in Park Street where, if you were a Do-It-Yourself man, you could go to him, tell him the sort of job you had in mind and he would sell you what you needed, even down to the exact number of screws required, and then often tell you how to do it as part of the bargain! Shopping was still a pleasure in those days, I regret to say that it has now become a soul-less task with so many shops, most of which are "multiples", having adopted the self-service principle of merchandising.

Early in 1960, Camberley's tradesmen became aware that the Council had appointed a firm of consultant architects, Messrs.Shingler & Risden, to produce a tentative plan for the comprehensive re-development of the whole central shopping area of the town (now called the Town Centre). This comprised the rectangular area bounded by Park Street, London Road, Knoll Road and the railway; i.e. Captain Raleigh Knight's original "Cambridge Town".

To enable such a plan to be put into being, as and when it had been approved, it would be necessary for the actual re-development area to be designated as liable to compulsory purchase by the Council to ensure that development could be achieved in accordance with the plan. We were also told that it would be a primary concern of the Council to seek to ensure that all traders and residents within this area should not be set at a disadvantage or prejudiced in any way, and that every effort would be made to that end.

The first sight that Camberley's shopkeepers had of their Council's Town Centre Re-development scheme was at a public meeting held at the Agincourt Hall, Yorktown, in May 1960, when the plan and a model of the proposed development was put on show. Amongst other proposals envisaged was a multi-storey car park sited near the railway, and the elimination of the existing central car park in Obelisk Street, with shops being built on this site. Two department stores were scheduled in the plans, and a high rise block of flats with shops below in Obelisk Street.

This plan did not meet with much approval from existing traders, who could see quite clearly that the removal of the central car park to a site near the railway, and the placement of other proposed car parks on the perimeter of the shopping area, would present very considerable trading advantages to the new shops that were to be built nearby, and that this would be particularly detrimental to shops sited in the London Road and the northern part of the High Street. That this fear was not unfounded, has been amply proved by subsequent events.

The Chamber of Trade set up a special sub-committee to carefully study these plans, and it was empowered to co-opt representatives from other interested organisations to serve on this committee. The Council chairman, Mr Rees, assured the chamber that his Council would "welcome considered opinions" and that he looked forward to future co-operation.

However, after several years of controversy, the Council's final plan for the area appeared in 1963, which ignored practically every one of the Chamber of Trade's suggestions, and those of other local organisations, and resulted in the Town Centre we have today. The cottages, school, car park and one or two shops that existed in the area between the High Street and Park Street were all demolished, and our present concrete shopping centre put in its place. Fortunately no high rise block of flats was ever built, but the traffic congestion problem still exists, and the associated car parking difficulties that are still experienced here prove that the plan adopted in 1963 was by no means the best that we could have had.

The actual building of the Town Centre was put out to tender by the Town Council, and the Arndale Development Company, a firm specialising in Town Centre Re-developments, secured the contract, by which they were granted long ground leases by the Council, who had previously compulsorily purchased most of the land required at completely un-inflated prices, fixed by the

Most of the area shown in this picture was demolished in 1963-5 to make way for our new Town Centre buildings. At the top near the word "Air" is the Staff College, and just below the London Road runs from left to right. The High Street is to the right and St.Georges Church can be seen. The National Primary School is left centre, with Obelisk Street just above. The open space to the left of the school became our central car park in the 50s. The cottages with their gardens in Princess Street at the bottom of the picture and those in Cross Street just above, built by Captain Knight in the 1860s, are visible, but Park Street is just out of the picture to the left. The shops and buildings lining the High Street and London Road were left intact, but the whole of the area enclosed by these two roads and Park Street were compulsorily purchased and then demolished to make way for the new Town Centre.

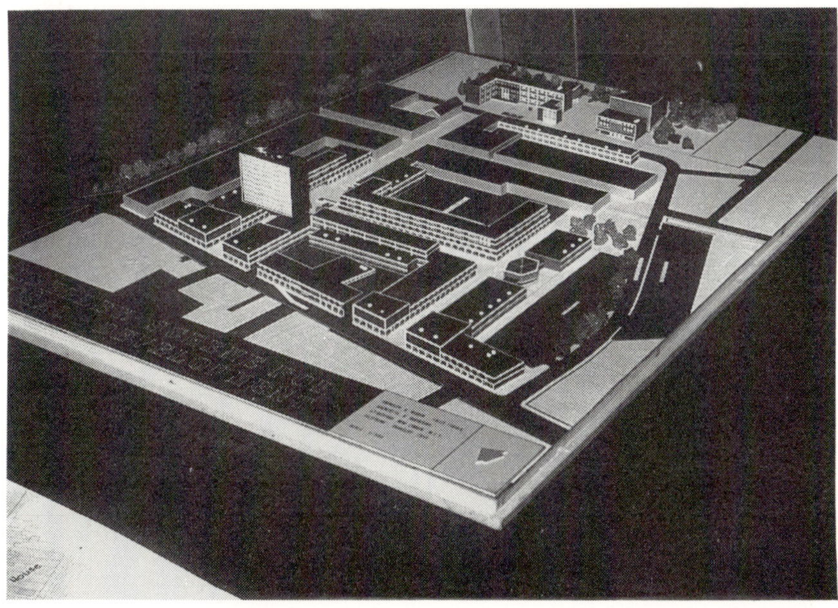

The model produced by Shingler & Risden at the public meeting of 1960. High Street at the top of the picture and Park Street at the bottom. The high rise block of flats proposed is to the left in Obelisk Street.

district valuer based on pre-development value figures. Arndale (now Town & City) and their partners in the venture, the Prudential, then became the landlords of most of the shops they built in the Town Centre, and they thus have a monopoly over the rental terms applicable to all the shops in this area for a very long time to come. The Council receives 40% of whatever is the current rent, but has to maintain the multi-storey car park and pedestrian ways. Was this a wise move on the part of our Council? Time alone will show!

During the 20 years that have followed the construction of the Town Centre, the Council have made their other dream come true. We now have the Library and Civic Hall built on the site of "Holmdale" in Knoll Road, and the Borough of Surrey Heath's new offices next to these where "Cambridge Villas/Woodbourne" once stood. Would it not be appropriate to see a statue of Captain Raleigh Knight, Cambridge Town's founder, erected in front of these offices? His was the mind that originally conceived the town's growth, and it would be nice to see him looking out at what has become of his creation.

Princess Street prior to re-development, looking towards the High Street. The site of the multi-storey car park is to the right of the picture.

The M3 being constructed through the Brackendale and Tekells Estates. Teams of bulldozers and graders being used to level the ground.

CHAPTER 27

The construction of the M3 commenced in 1965 and continued on until 1972, when the Camberley section was opened for traffic.

During this period the Warren Estate had been completed and also the Watchetts Estate, save for a portion close to the Motorway. The targets for the building development companies now became the estates of Camberley's landed gentry - "Frimley Hall", "Elsenwood", "Graitney", "Eastlea Court", "Edmonscote", "Collingwood Park" and "Heatherside".

World War II had greatly impoverished many of these families and made the maintenance of their large houses, with roofing of an intricate pattern, an almost impossible task. Frequent repairs were needed, none of which had been done during the war owing to the shortage of skilled labour, and their once beautiful gardens had become wildernesses for the same reason. All these houses had been designed in the days when labour was plentiful, and they required a staff of anything from 5-10 servants to maintain them properly. To make things still more difficult, most of their kitchens had no labour-saving devices, and were often situated well away from the living rooms of the house.

During the war nearly all of Camberley's domestic servants had been called up for war service of one form or another, and the sense of independence that this had given them made most of them unwilling to return to this sort of employment after the war. Gardeners were virtually unobtainable, and getting any sort of house repairs done became a nightmare. Those with small houses found this difficult enough, but it was ten times harder for the owner of a big house. Therefore, they rapidly declined, for only a very few could find either the labour or the money to keep them up. This was especially so for those ladies who had become widowed during the war.

The only post-war solution that seemed to be open to those of Camberley's landed gentry who wished to keep their houses, was either to convert them into flats, or try to sell off part of the gardens for building. But this was not easy as, until the 1960's, there was not a great demand for land in Camberley. In any case, one had first to obtain all sorts of planning permission from the Council and then overcome the many restraints on building imposed by our immediate post-war Government, in order to be able to carry out any alterations to one's house. In addition, those who sold land had to pay the Government a considerable "Development Charge" as a tax on the transaction, and this was not abolished until many years later.

The other alternative was to try to find a buyer for the whole estate, including the house, but in the 50's few had any inkling of the developments that were to come, and speculators who were prepared to demolish the house, and then "sit on" the land for years to come until it could be re-sold, were hard to find.

Almost the only people who were interested in buying complete estates at that period were the Education Authorities, or the Principals of Private Schools and Private Nursing Homes, and several were bought for this purpose. "Edmonscote" became Ravenscote School and the Teachers Training Centre - "Graitney" became Crawley Ridge Middle School - "Tomlinscote", Tomlinscote

Camberley in 1958

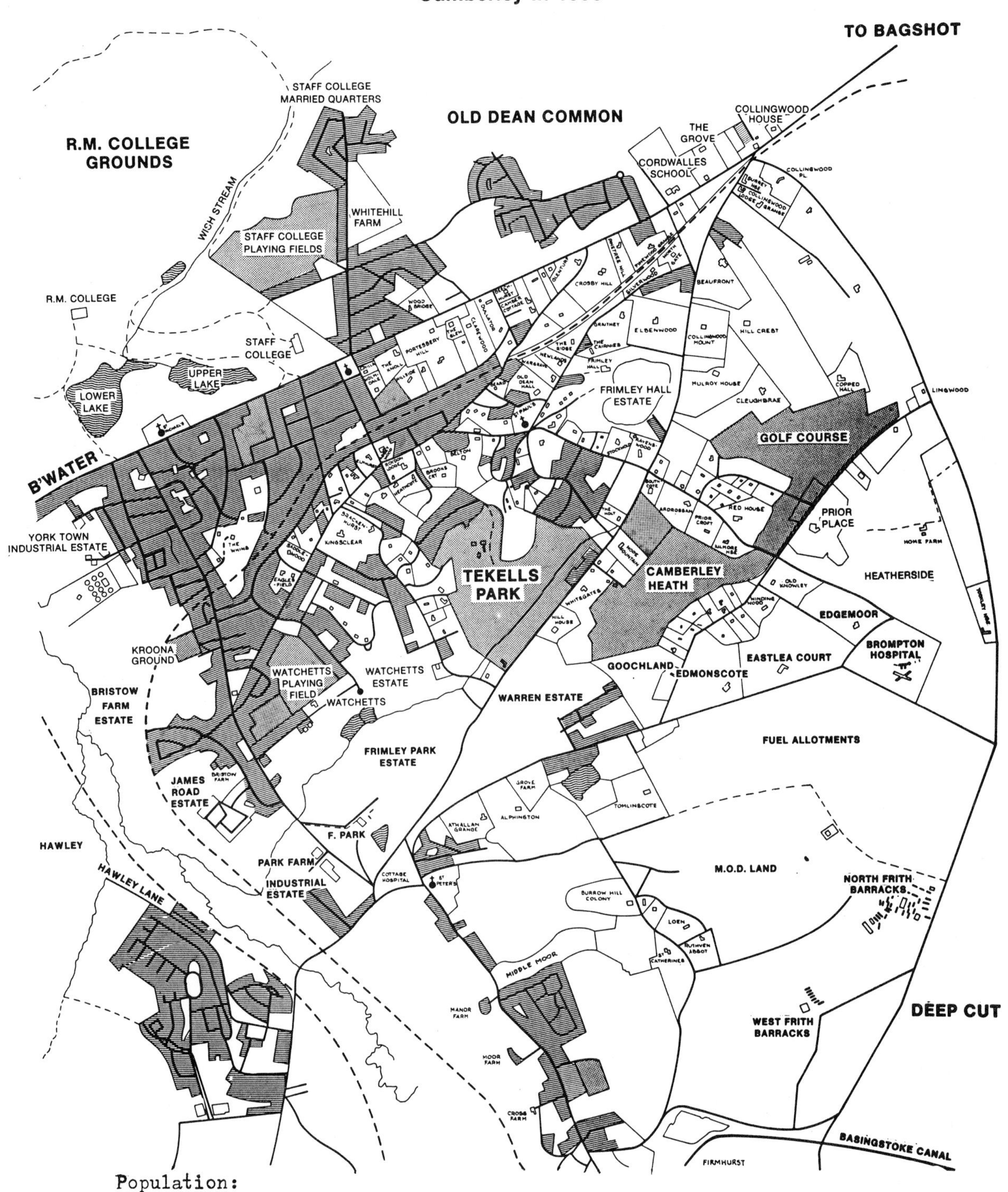

Population:

1958 - 24,500 est.

Industrial development had started in Camberley during WW2 and by 1958 there were 32 firms located on the Yorktown Industrial Estate and on Park Farm. A Private housing building firm bought the Warren Estate and commenced to develop it and the Watchetts Estate was 2/3rds complete. A new Council housing Estate was built on Old Dean Common and another around James Road on Bristow Farm. In Frimley the first of the Manor Farms also had a Council housing Estate built around Worsley Road. In Hampshire, across the Blackwater River another Industrial Estate was commenced in Hawley Lane and many houses built as well. Our "Overspill" population had not yet started to arrive and most of our 'Landed Gentry'S' estates had not been sold to housing developers.

Camberley Developments constructed between 1958-1970 whilst M3 was under construction

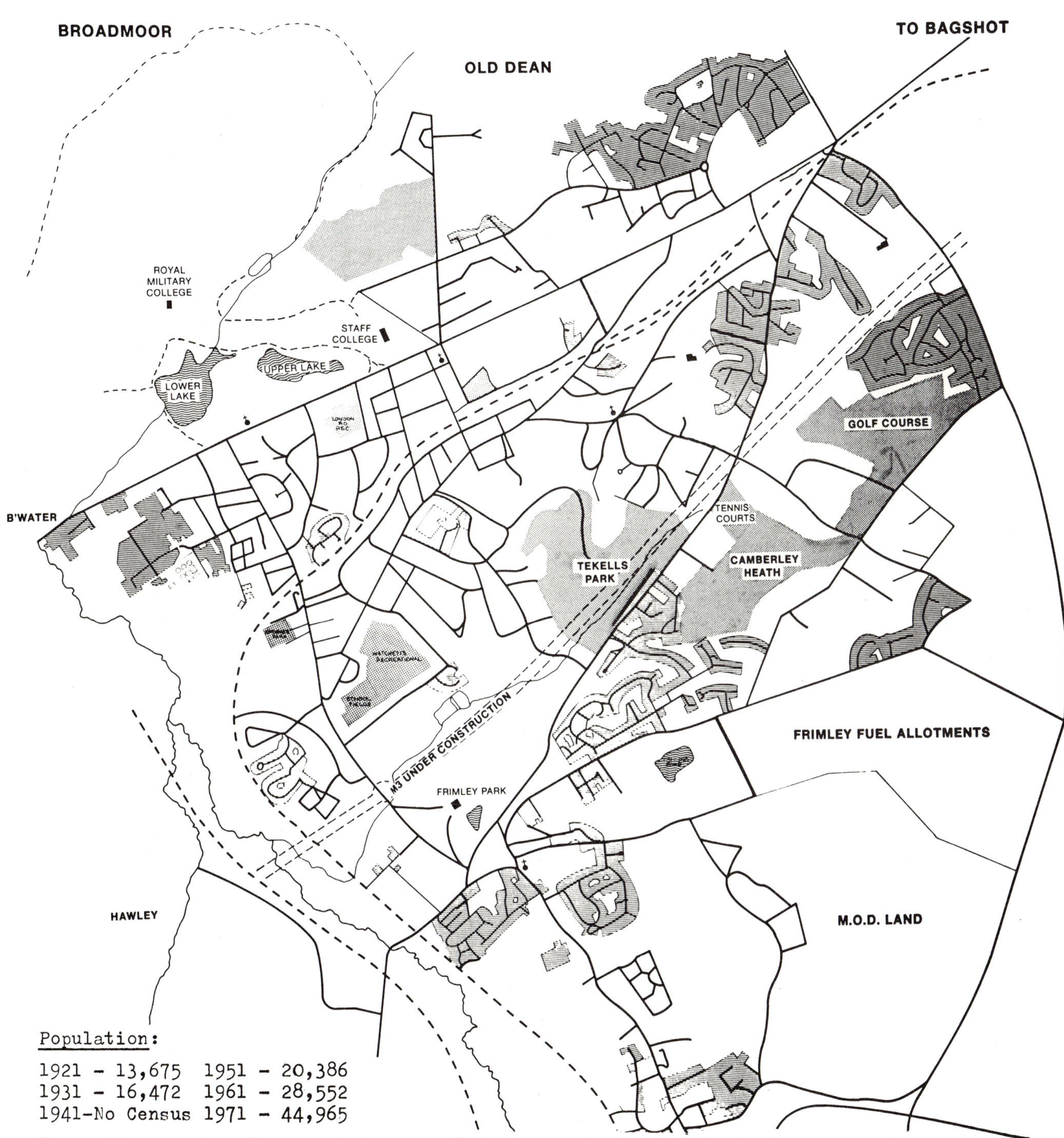

Population:

1921 - 13,675 1951 - 20,386
1931 - 16,472 1961 - 28,552
1941-No Census 1971 - 44,965

These figures show the great impetus that the arrival of Camberley's "Overspill" new residents made to our growth from 1958 onwards. This spurred on our Industrial development and an added factor was the commencement of work on the construction of the M3 Motorway in 1968. Private housing developments rapidly got under way on the Warren Estate and at Whitegates, Kingsclear, Frimley Hall, Elsenwood, Eastlea Court, and Copped Hall. Building also commenced at Beaufront, Hillcrest, and Collingwood Place in Collingwood Park; at The Whins on the France Hill Estate; The Priory in Frimley village and at Alphington on the Chobham Road. Council housing estates were built for our Overspill residents on Old Dean Common and James Road in Camberley and another farm in Frimley became the Ansell Road Estate. Yorktown Industrial Estate was extended and Park Farm Industrial Estate commenced. In Frimley, the Johnsons factory was built near the Blackwater River at Middle Moor in 1965.

County Secondary School - "The Grove and Cordwalles", Collingwood Secondary School - "Lhasa/Ardrossan", Prior Heath First School - "Broomfield", St.Catherine's Preparatory School - and "France Hill House", France Hill Secondary School.

"Frimley Hall" had been sold to the Spears family a few years before the war. They were builders who specialised in quality housing and in the conversion of old timbered buildings to modern usage without the destruction of their character. The Old Barn by the side of the Cambridge Hotel was an example of their work in this respect. They turned the Hall into a hotel with one of the family in charge, and commenced the development of the estate by constructing Lime Avenue and Crawley Drive. But only a few houses had been built there when war came, and work had to cease.

About 1950 they sold the hotel to Mr and Mrs Shepherd who, amongst other improvements that they innovated there, held Dinner-Dances for young 'Camberley'. Their son, David Shepherd, is the artist who has achieved so much fame with his Elephant and Big-game pictures of African wild life. At one time, a mural that he painted when he was a boy, depicting an underwater scene of fishes swimming round a coral reef, occupied the whole of one wall of the Entrance Hall of the hotel. Many years later, when Trust House Forte bought the hotel, this was found stored away in the loft and was returned to David at a little handing-over ceremony, when he in turn presented them with a framed elephant print, with a suitable plaque beneath, which now hangs in the hotel.

One Christmas, just after I had been married, David asked me to display two of his paintings in my salon to see if I could sell them for him, priced at £20 each. They were beautiful river scenes of London and I badly wanted one of these for myself, but our "newly-wed" house needed furniture even more. So, very sadly, I had to pass up the chance to own a "David Shepherd" original, painted at the time when he was an unknown artist! Later, he got his first real break when he obtained permission to go to Heathrow to paint pictures of aircraft on the ground. He then hung his aviation pictures in the lounge of the hotel in the hope of getting buyers, particularly at Farnborough Air Show week when the hotel was packed with people attending the event. Later an exhibition of his work at Heathrow assisted in getting his career going, to the delight of all those who knew him in Camberley.

The Shepherds retired from hotel-keeping a few years later and since then the hotel has had several owners and undergone a few alterations, but the exterior of the house is still much as it was when Mr Wright occupied it in the 20's. However, the park in which he had his little private golf course is no more, and is now the site of Paddock Close and the nearby side roads, which were built about 1960. The estate was developed with some very nice houses, most of which had enough ground for a decent sized garden to be made. The hotel is now owned by Trust House Forte.

The "Elsenwood" estate came on to the market in 1953 after the death of Brigadier Van der Byl, whose soldiering family had owned the house from the time that it was built in 1885. Highclere Drive and Elsenwood Crescent were built on this land, but the house was demolished.

"Graitney", once the home of Vice-Admiral Johnstone, and subsequently owned by Mr James Cubitt, an architect, was sold to the County Council in 1960 for a school to be built there. F. & C.U.D.C. then wished to purchase this land from them and turn it into a public park, but were unable to persuade them to sell. At that time, the gardens were in a fine condition but, by the time the school was eventually built a year or two later, much damage had been done to them by vandals. By a strange coincidence, Mr Cubitt's aunt was married to Sir Robert Watson-Smyth, who also sold his house, "The Grove", to the County Council for Barossa Secondary School - both houses being demolished in the process.

"Eastlea Court" had been owned by the Astleys from 1905 until about 1928, when it was bought by an American family. But just before World War II it was burnt down and a new "Eastlea Court" was built by them in a different part of their estate. I am told by the present owner of this house, Mr Terry Lyons, that when the new house was first built the American lady found it had been incorrectly sited to get the sun into the living rooms. So it was all pulled down and rebuilt facing in a different direction to obviate this fault, but after this was done, its owners still did not like it and so they sold it and went back to America.

During World War II it was used to house soldiers, and afterwards it was divided into two parts, one of which was occupied by Barbara Moore, the famous Russian lady walker, and the other by Major-General Buchanan-Dunlop. They had a most acrimonious dispute over their rights there terminating in a very costly law suit. Eventually Barbara Moore left Camberley and not long afterwards committed suicide. Holly Avenue now surrounds the site of the first "Eastlea Court", whilst Westerdale Road leads to the second "Eastlea Court". Fern Close is also on a part of the original estate.

Left: Frimley Hall, built by Mr G.W.Fowler in 1882, is an hotel owned by Trust House Forte. It once had a small "pitch and putt" golf course in the Park.

Below: David Shepherd, as a young man, at work on one of his aviation pictures at Heathrow and the notice of the first exhibition of his painting held in London in 1955.

THE FIRST LONDON EXHIBITION
OF
AERONAUTICAL, INDUSTRIAL AND LANDSCAPE

PAINTINGS
BY
DAVID SHEPHERD, S.Av.A.

OPENING BY
SIR MILES THOMAS, D.F.C.

ON MONDAY, 3RD OCTOBER, 1955
AT 3 P.M.,
PARSONS GALLERY
70 GROSVENOR STREET, NEW BOND STREET, W.1.
(Kindly lent by Thos. Parsons & Sons Ltd.)

THE EXHIBITION REMAINS OPEN UNTIL OCTOBER 21ST, 1955.
HOURS: 10 a.m.-5 p.m. Daily (Saturdays and Sundays excepted)
10 a.m.-8 p.m. on Mon. 3rd, Thurs. 6th, Tues. 11th and Fri. 21st.

Air Vice-Marshall Sir John Cordingley, K.C.B., C.B.E., R.A.F. (ret'd.) will introduce Sir Miles Thomas.

THE ROYAL AIR FORCE BENEVOLENT FUND
WILL BENEFIT FROM THE EXHIBITION.

3

CHAPTER 28

Whilst there had been some doubts as to the exact route that the M3 was to take through Camberley, there had been a lull in building developments in Collingwood Park and the Royal Albert Orphanage grounds. From the moment that this was resolved work commenced on these Estates.

The Motorway had divided the Royal Albert Orphanage land (now the W.R.A.C. College) into two parts, in the southern half of which was "Copped Hall", an estate of 10 acres which ran alongside the 9th fairway of Camberley Heath Golf Course, the house being reached by a long drive through a wood, starting from the Maultway. It had once been owned by Captain Vivian Loyd and had a large paddock in front of the house in which he kept several hunters. I am told that when he sold the estate for £25,000 he thought he had done very well, and he nearly had a heart attack when he found it had been re-sold for £250,000 only a few months later. Another 35 acres of the surrounding woodland was now added to its original 10, so that the Copped Hall Estate now stretched from the Maultway to the neighbouring Clewborough Estate. To the south it adjoined "Lingwood", once owned by Count de Salis, but this estate was not built upon until 1986. The area is a pleasant one in which to live, despite a certain amount of noise from the M3, and within the space of the next ten years the estate became almost fully developed with up-market houses, the majority of which were individually architect designed.

There is a separate estate in the N.E. corner of the W.R.A.C. grounds of about 20 acres, in which "Surrey House" and "Collingwood Lodge" had been built about 1870. Two more houses had been added to the estate in Edwardian times, "Collingwood Grange" and "Collingwood Place", and another, "Bagshot Heath" ("Green Meadows") built on a smaller adjoining estate which abutted Collingwood Farm. The 3 Collingwood Houses all belonged to members of the Mackenzie family, one of whom was married to Colonel Uzielli who owned "Surrey House". After World War II all but one of these houses had been converted into flats, but I am glad to be able to record that they have all survived and provide us with some fine examples of the houses in which Camberley's landed gentry once lived. About 1965, Maultway Crescent and Foxhill Crescent were built in the grounds of these houses situated in the highest part of Camberley. (Map, Page 112)

The Collingwood Park Estate, situated between the W.R.A.C. College and the Portsmouth Road and now bounded to the south by the Motorway, comprised an area of about 100 acres and was still in its original 5 Estates in 1965, although a few houses had been built in their gardens here and there.

"Hillcrest" (now called Collingwood Hall) was the first of these estates to be broken up. Situated on Colling Ridge, the house commanded a fine view all round and in its grounds had a Bowling Alley and Stables, over which there was a Clock Tower. Two driveways led to the house, which lay back some 300 yards from the Portsmouth Road. One of these became Hillcrest Road which commenced the estate's development, and the other Chatsworth Heights, the two roads being joined up on the Ridge where "Hillcrest" house had once stood. I am glad to say that the modern housing developers who have built the houses on this beautiful site have not betrayed their trust, and have built houses worthy of their locality. (Photograph, Page 46)

In between "Hillcrest's" two driveways was the "Beaufront" Estate of

Residential Camberley Developments made between 1970 & 1985 after M3 was opened

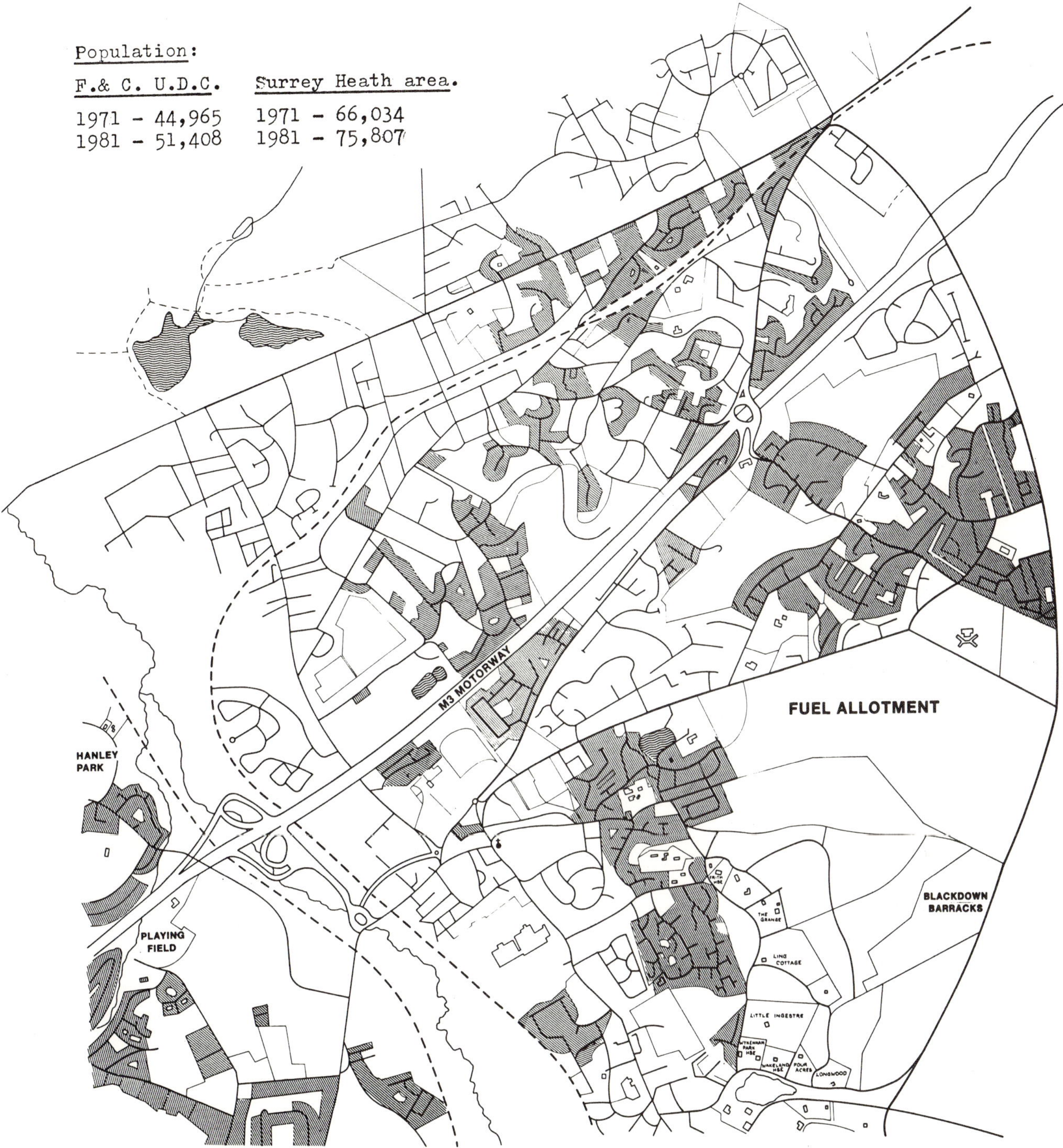

The M3 was opened in 1972 to give an added spur to Camberley's growth. Most of the remaining houses of our 'Landed Gentry' were soon demolished to make way for new private housing developments. In this way, Belton, Shalbourne, Waverley Court, Stockwood, Collingwood Mount, Mulroy House, Wargrave, The Ridge, Red House, Lhasa, and Ardrossan all in the Church Hill/Crawley Ridge area disappeared together with Crosby Hill, Pinewood Grange and Carlinwark on the London Road. A new estate was built on Parkside near the new Frimley Park hospital and the Watchetts and Pine Wood Estates extended. The 250 acre Heatherside Estate was developed as a separate community with its own Centre and shops. In Frimley and Frimley Green, Bowling Green Farm, Moor Farm and Cross Farm were all built upon as were the areas close to St. Catherines and Burrow Hill. Around Tomlins Pond the Alphington Estate was completed and Tomlinscote School built. The Industrial Estates of Yorktown and Park Farm were completed and those of Albany Park, Athallan Grange and the Frimley Business Park commenced . By 1985 the old F.& C. U.D.C.'s estimated population was around 55,000.

some 15 acres. The house, which had alternated between being called "Maywood" and "Beaufront", had been partly burnt down during the early years of World War II, and only the ground floor left standing. About 1940, the Army had requisitioned the house for use by the A.T.S. and it was during their occupancy that it is said someone left an iron on in one of the bedrooms and this caused the fire, which was not noticed until a parlourmaid in "Elsenwood", on the other side of the Portsmouth Road, saw that the upper storey of "Beaufront" was on fire and raised the alarm.

A private road leads to the house, and beyond it to a wooden building that was once the chapel of Beaufront School and has since been converted into a dwelling house surrounded by a beautiful garden.

During the year 1944, our Queen, who was then Princess Elizabeth, learnt to drive Army Vehicles on this road when she was in the A.T.S. I have been given a most delightful account of her training course at "Beaufront" when she was just 18 years old. This was written by Mrs Ashton-Rose, who was a Driving and Maintenance Instructor there at that time. She recounts those days in these words:

"When the Queen came for three weeks, a special course was set up consisting of NCO's, so that she should be part of a class rather than be taught on her tod! She had officer instructors, which was a shame, because normally they never did any teaching - just went around sitting in on us normal instructors and generally inhibit us, because it is very true to say that they didn't know nearly as much as we did!

Nevertheless, the Princess, as she was then, revelled in every minute. She was so 'liberated' as there wasn't a single lady-in-waiting or bodyguard - something she had never experienced before. Lady Violet Wellesley, our Company Commander, had the sole responsibility for her and used to drive over to Windsor Castle every morning. Elizabeth would drive back to "Beaufront", and then back to the Castle in the evening, which was part of her driving practice. She did her maintenance instruction in the forecourt of the chauffeur's garages, so I had a first class view from the window of my flat above. My happiest memory of her is of her first day, dressed in dungarees with a scarf on her head, tied factory-girl fashion, taking surreptitious, horrified looks at her greasy hands!

There used to be fifteen minutes interval between all lectures, principally because we seemed to have to change our clothes for almost every different function, and, if there was time and the weather was fine, the Princess used to join us on the slope outside the sitting room and chat. It was difficult to remember who she was as she fitted in so well. As you can imagine, there was a lot of aircraft traffic from Farnborough, and she would lie on her back, shading her eyes with her hands, and give us chapter and verse on each different plane that went over. Apparently the King was very keen to teach her aircraft recognition! She used to tell us how he would inspect her every morning before she left the Castle to make sure that she was properly dressed, shoes shined and buttons gleaming! He nearly every day told her to wipe off some of her lipstick and the first thing she used to do on arrival was to go up to the room that had been put at her disposal and replace the lipstick - we could see her through the window!

I think the most amazing thing of all during that period was the total security that prevailed. We were all given a pep-talk before she arrived on how to behave, and above all keep our mouths shut. Do you know, I don't believe any one at all disobeyed. Isn't that incredible for quite a large

The Queen, or Princess Elizabeth as she then was, with a group of ATS girls undergoing their driving instruction course in the grounds of Beaufront. Car maintenance was part of the course.

Beaufront House. A girls' Boarding School until the start of World War II. First called Mayfield School, then Beaufront School. After it had been requisitioned by the Army for the ATS, the School moved to Mulroy House. During World War II, the upper storey was destroyed by fire.

number of women from all walks of life and differing standards of integrity. There were NEVER any sightseers outside the gates and, on the day she left, when we had a bit of a party and escorted her car right out into the road, giving her a hearty cheer, there was not a single civilian to be seen. Unbelievable!"

When "Beaufront" was requisitioned, the school was removed to "Mulroy House" further down the Portsmouth Road, which was bought by Beaufront School Limited for this purpose. This was the house that had once belonged to the Spanish ambassador. However, when the Motorway was being built, Miss Richards and Miss Creed, who then owned the school, decided to close the school and move it to Dorset as they thought that the noise of the M3 would be too great for study in such close proximity. Indeed, a slice of their estate was required for the Motorway to be constructed, and both this and "Mulroy House" estate were sold for development at the same time. Mulroy Avenue now leads to the site occupied by the house, now demolished, which was on the right hand side of the road. The very long part of the estate bordering the M3 is now Iberian Way, but the houses at its extreme eastern end are actually on a bit of the old "Hillcrest" estate, and not on the "Mulroy" estate which adjoins it at this point.

"Cleughbrae" (now called Clewborough) was the sole Collingwood Park house to survive, and its estate remained intact for a further 20 years until 1986. It was built about 1901 as a private residence for Major-General England. In 1913 it was occupied by the Hon. N.M.Farrer then, during World War I, it was used as an officers' convalescent home. During World War II it was taken over by the Free French for use by their agents on their return from occupied France. After the war it was divided into flats and remained so until 1968, when it was converted into Clewborough House Preparatory School by Lt.Col. D.A.R.Clarke, the principal of the school. It is a most gracious looking house and at one end it has a conical tower, and so was almost certainly designed by Mr Poulter, the architect.

The estate, however, has now been much reduced in size, so that the school has only 2½ acres surrounding it left of its original 20-30 acres. First the Motorway, which runs lengthwise through the northern side of the estate, sliced off 8-10 acres and then, in 1986, about half of the remainder became a housing development along Youlden Way, with their gardens running alongside the 6th fairway of Camberley Heath. There is still another portion of the estate which has as yet not been built upon alongside the 9th hole. It is heavily wooded with pine trees and is, no doubt, the depository of a number of golf balls well and truly hooked off the 9th tee - some of mine amongst them!

The school has a delightful open-air swimming pool and a tennis court by the side of the house. Looking at it from across the spacious lawns in front one can get some idea of the splendid life-style that our wealthy Camberley landed gentry enjoyed in Victorian and Edwardian times.

Clewborough House
Preparatory School
1986

CHAPTER 29

The 1950's and 60's saw the further development of the Watchetts Estate. A number of new houses were built in Parkway and Watchetts Drive, and the "Watchetts" House" was demolished to make way for Watchetts Lake Close. Then Park Avenue and Kingsley Avenue were constructed, joined together by Linkway, and by 1965 all these roads were fully developed, the building plots of 1/3rd to 1/2 an acre ensuring that all houses built on the Watchetts Estate would have pleasant gardens. The constrictive covenants in the land conveyances, originally inserted by Mr Verran in 1929, were enforced in the development of the estate, whereby only houses as distinct to bungalows could be erected, and all of these had to be of a certain minimum specified value. Mr Verran gave what had once been the pleasure gardens of "Watchetts House" to the Camberley Cricket Club, and they turned this into a fine cricket ground, building a pavilion there. The stables belonging to the house were not demolished and some land surrounding this was made into a Nursery Garden, which continued until the late 70's. After the opening of the M3, Parkway was continued on towards the Motorway as Verran Road, and another new housing estate made bordering the M3 running eastwards to join up with the Brackendale Estate.

By the time the Motorway was completed, Camberley was in desperate need of another hospital. The population explosion that had occurred both here and in the surrounding neighbourhoods meant that a large General Hospital was required. Land was found for this just south of the M3 in the grounds of "Frimley Park Manor House", and the hospital was built and officially opened by Barbara Castle, the then Minister of Health, in 1975. A row of small semi-detached houses was also built in Gilbert Road nearby for occupation by the hospital staff. But, already in 1986, the hospital is unable to cope with our district's huge population expansion and more ground is to be utilised for its extension by further inroads upon what is still left of "Frimley Park Manor House's" pleasure gardens.

The strip of Frimley Park Estate to the east of the hospital that lay between Portsmouth Road and the Motorway became the Parkside Housing Estate. Pans Gardens and Tekels Way were later constructed in the part of the Brackendale and Tekells Estates cut off when the M3 was built through their property.

Camberley Heath Golf Club had been in financial difficulties in the 50's owing to the necessity arising for urgent repairs to the Club House and the escalation in the running costs of such a large establishment. To raise the required sum, the Directors of Camberley Heath Limited decided to sell off the tennis courts and croquet lawns belonging to the club, as building land. At about the same time, "Whitegates", whose land ran along Golf Drive, also sold off part of their grounds for building and this area was jointly developed. A further part of their land, adjacent to the Warren Estate, became Wilmot Way. The membership of Camberley Heath was also in need of extension in order to ensure its financial viability in the future, and so the 50 members of the "Artisan" section of the club were offered the opportunity to become full playing members. Most accepted, thus saving it from being sold to "outside bodies". Dr Hartley, the well known eye specialist, was the club's captain at the time and his genial personality was a great factor in the warm welcome that was accorded to all the club's new members. There is a bench by the side of the 10th tee put there in his memory to remind the club of what they owe to him for his efforts on their behalf in the difficult 50's.

In the 60's and 70's, the Pine Woods Estate continued its development along Walkers Ridge, where a number of delightful houses were built. On the other half of the Estate, "Belton House" was demolished and Bellever Hill and Deepwell Drive took its place. Yeomans Way now connects the two parts of the original Pine Woods Estate of 1892. "Belton House" was at the top of quite a steep portion of Crawley Ridge, and leading up to it from Park Road were the grounds of "Shalbourne" and another neighbouring house "Ochiltree" which was one of several being utilised to board pupils attending Elmhurst Ballet School in the 60's, but the school had by now become so successful that a decision had been made to build boarding accommodation for all their pupils under one roof on their Heathcote Road property. They also decided to construct their own Elmhurst Theatre on land nearby. "Ochiltree" was, therefore, sold and the Shalbourne Rise estate built there.

In Crawley Ridge Road, "Old Dean Hall" was converted into the Tudor Hall block of flats, "Wargrave" and "The Ridge" became Ashwell Avenue, and several of the Branksome Park Road houses sold their gardens for building. Along the approach road to Frimley Hall some elegant houses appeared and also a few more in Crawley Drive.

Off Portesbery Road, Langley Drive and Clarewood Drive were constructed in the grounds of "Sarsdenfield" and "Clarewood", the Edwardian houses being preserved. In Middleton Road, "Crosby Hall" and "Carlinwark" fell into the hands of the developers to be replaced by a sizeable housing estate. Similarly, "Pinewood Grange" by Larchwood Glade. Many of the other London Road houses sold portions of their large gardens for building, but most were preserved, amongst which were "High Ridding" and "St.Annes". (Map, Page 117)

"Glenturf" is also still there, notable to the historian because it has a well in its grounds under which the Cam Stream flows on its underground passage from Old Dean Common to the Blackwater River, crossing the High Street, Park Street and Belmont Road en route. When the foundations were being excavated for the large store in Park Street that R.P.Over and Sons occupied until quite recently, the builders unexpectedly hit the Cam Stream and this caused such problems for them that they eventually had to abandon the project for others to complete at a later date.

On the northern side of London Road, Diamond Hill Road was made and houses built alongside. The Army also extended its Staff College officers quarters at Barossa by the addition of several new Closes. Whitehill Farm nearby is the last piece of agricultural land that exists in Camberley, but I understand that this too may disappear before long.

Towards the end of the 70's practically all the re-development of the "landed gentry's" old estates that could be done appeared to have taken place, and the only two that were still left undeveloped were the W.R.A.C. College (Royal Albert Orphanage) and the 250 acre Heatherside Estate which had belonged to the Goldney family ever since they foreclosed on Mongredien when he went bankrupt in 1875. They had built "Prior Place" there, and had had a succession of tenant farmers on their Home Farm and managers on Heatherside Nurseries. They had also sold 30 acres of the Estate to Brompton Hospital. "Prior Place" was now a private sanatorium known as the Baldwin Brown Convalescent Home.

In the late 70's all of the Heatherside Estate, with the exception of

"Prior Place", "Heatherside House", "Brompton Hospital" and a 30 acre site to the east of the hospital, was sold to the Bovis Homes Co. for development.

Several hundred "middle-market" homes were built there, with Cumberland Road running through the centre of the estate. Goldney Road had been made by the family in the 1880's (they had also installed gas lighting at their own expense in Prior Road in the 20's to light the approach to Heatherside), but it still remains a gravel road to this day. Near to this, Winding Wood Road was constructed and houses built there on the Edmonscote Estate land.

The Heatherside Estate is the biggest single private housing estate in Camberley and has its own school, shopping and community centres, all of which have combined to make it a self-contained neighbourhood unit. The fine Wellingtonia Avenue of trees has been preserved and "Yockley House", "Prior Place", "Heatherside House" and "Millbrook House" are all still there. The 30 acre site next to Brompton Hospital has now been developed with high density housing and is called the "Cheylesmore Park", named after the Lord Lieutenant of Surrey present at the opening of Brompton Sanatorium.

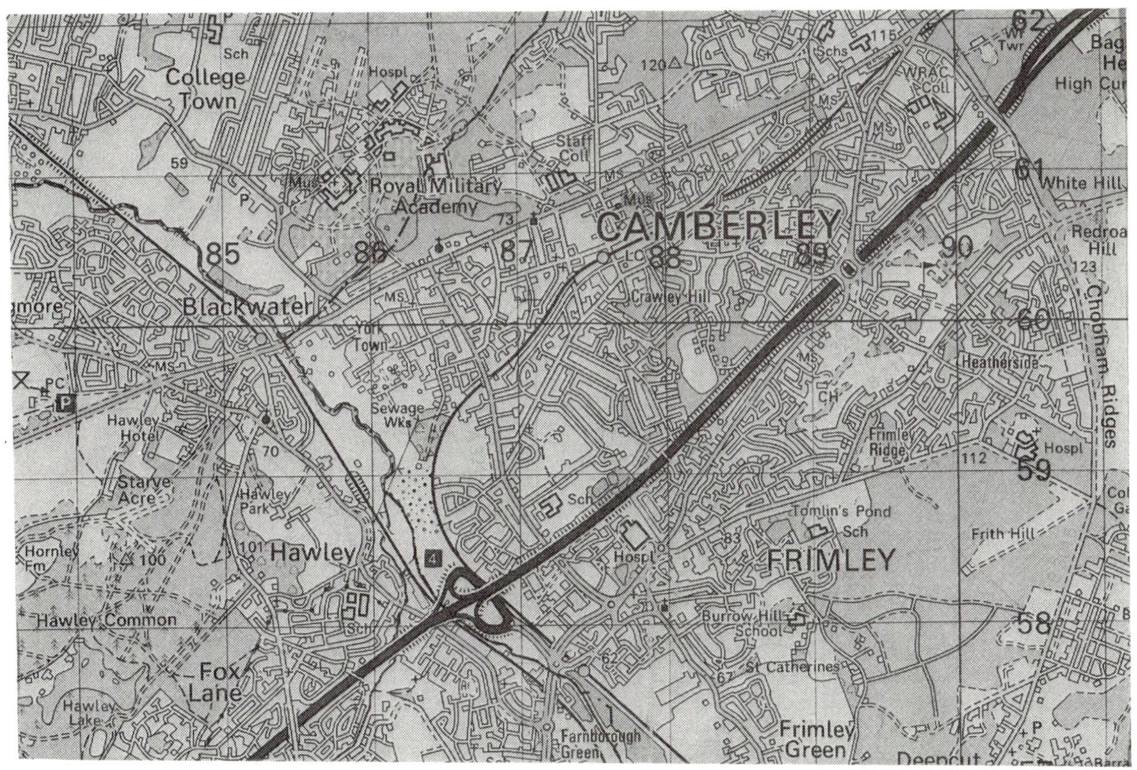

Camberley and her Neighbours in 1982.
The Residential Area now completely built-up except for the W.R.A.C. College
The only open spaces left are Tekells Park, Camberley Heath Golf Course, the School's Playing Fields, Krooner Park and the Watchetts and London Road Recreation Grs. Three of the Frimley/Frimley Green farms have as yet not been built upon.

The Blackwater Valley Road was planned, but not yet constructed, or the further Industrial Developments along this road. The continuation through the fields of Sandhurst Park and College Farm, together with housing developments alongside, was started 3 years later.

The considerable developments which had occurred at Frogmore Park in Blackwater and in Hawley and Cove can be seen. Hawley Park and the Army Estates at Minley and near Hawley Lake provide the only "Breathing Spaces" on the opposite side of the Blackwater River to Camberley and Frimley.

CHAPTER 30

The first school in Camberley was situated opposite to "Tea Caddy Row" in Yorktown on the site now occupied by Trend Homecentre Warehouse. It was a "National School" which had been established in 1818 and was for boys and girls.

In 1811 the (Anglican) National Society for promoting the education of the poor in the principles of the Established Church was founded and their schools were called National Schools. In addition to teaching the three "R's", their curriculum included such activities as tailoring, cobbling, gardening and agriculture for boys, and sewing, knitting, lace-making and baking for girls. Attendance at these schools was voluntary but in 1862 government grants became payable to them, based upon the attendance of children up to 12 years of age. Schools then had to keep log books, and in Yorktown National School there were 40 boys and 14 girls.

In 1864 a second National School was started in Cambridge Town attended chiefly by some 50-60 children of officers and civilian employees of the newly established Staff College, but I have been unable to ascertain just where this school was located.

The need for newer and larger buildings for the Yorktown School soon became apparent, and in January 1871 the pupils were transferred to a new school built on a site near to St.Michaels Church, on land given to them by the R.M.C. The school cost £1,400, which was raised from public subscriptions, donations and by a grant from the National Society.

Forster's Elementary Education Act had been passed in 1870 by Parliament. This established Primary Education for all, and set up District School Boards throughout the country charged with the duty of seeing that there was sufficient accommodation in public elementary schools for all children not otherwise provided for educationally. This necessitated the building of many new schools to supplement those voluntarily existing at that period, and if the latter category was not deemed to provide satisfactorily for the needs of a district, then a School Board would be set up there to do so. The School Boards were to be popularly elected from local dignitaries. In the National Schools, Church teaching was to be continued, but the new Board Schools were not to be used for Religious teaching, Catechism, or any denominational teaching.

The Board system was late in arriving in the Frimley parish; it was not established here until 1883, when the Frimley School Board was set up. Presumably the National Society was well able, until that time, to provide for the educational needs of the community. Certainly the Catholics in the area had made their own provision by building a school in Obelisk Street for 120 children in 1873.

When the Frimley Board was established, it took over the management of the Yorktown National School and that of Cambridge Town, and in 1887 they commenced the building of a new school for the latter in School Lane. This was for infants only who, at the age of 6, left to finish their schooling in Yorktown. But, in 1897, the Board erected a school for the higher age range next to the infant school, fronting on to Princess Street.

The 1870 Forster Act related only to Primary education and soon it was realised that there was no bridge to Higher education. In 1900, under the Cockerton Judgement, it was decided that ratepayers' money should be spent on Higher and Secondary education. Also parochial School Boards were becoming something of a problem. The 1902 Education Act dispensed with these and instead gave the power to provide both Primary and Secondary education to the elected County Councils and to the larger Borough Councils.

Separate Secondary education was slow starting in this locality. The need for a Secondary school of our own did not really become an urgent matter for public concern until the 1920's, by which time our population had grown to about 13,500. Some of the Council's elementary schools were giving a limited number of children a "Higher Grade" training, but any candidates who won Grammar School places had to journey to Woking, Farnham or Egham where there were Grammar Schools.

In 1929, with the development of the Watchetts Estate residentially by Mr Nicholas Verran, a site for a Secondary school, to be named the "Frimley and Camberley County School", was purchased fronting on to Frimley Road, and the school opened in 1931 with 40 pupils.

Of course, these State schools were not the only schools in Camberley at that time. There were also a number of private schools (see page 96), but this Chapter is concerned with Camberley's State schools and with our other early school, St.Tarcisius. This latter had expanded into two parts, the infants located in Obelisk Street and the junior school in a building in Charles Street situated behind the Church, where they remained until 1960, when they acquired Knoll House for their junior school and, a few years later, the old Yorktown National School buildings for their infants school, now known as St.Gregory's.

The 1944 Butler Education Act changed the educational scene drastically. It demanded that secondary education be made available by the authorities for all children, and the Elementary system gave way to the Infant and Junior schools. As a result of this, and the town's expanding population, France Hill Secondary Modern School was founded in 1947 in France Hill House, (Viscount Southwell's old home; once New Farm), which had previously been occupied by war time refugees from Croydon.

In 1958, the "Overspill" population of Camberley had started to arrive and the rapid expansion of our town's schooling facilities became a pressing necessity. A site in Watchetts Drive was acquired by the County Council and France Hill School was moved there into new, purpose-built premises capable of accommodating over 1,000 pupils. For a time the old France Hill House premises were occupied as an annexe to the new school but, soon after, these were taken over by the Camberley Adult Education Centre.

The new "Overspill" population also strained our Primary educational facilities to the limit and beyond. Pupils were being brought to the School Lane and Princess Street schools each day by special buses from the new estate on Old Dean Common. This pressure was partly relieved by the building of a new Primary school at the Grove in Chobham Road, Frimley, to which some of the pupils were transferred, and an Infants school was added to this in 1962.

In 1964-5, work on the new Town Centre commenced and this involved the demolition of both of our original State schools in School Lane and the Catholic school in Obelisk Street. The Catholics then took over the old Yorktown school premises and the Yorktown school moved to the James Road estate where it became Bristow School. In 1968 the Primary school children from School Lane were re-housed, the infants going to new temporary buildings behind France Hill House pending the building of a new school there, and the older children were transferred to what had been, until that moment, Camberley Grammar School's premises in Frimley Road - this is now the Watchetts Middle School.

The schooling requirements that arose through the building of the Old Dean Estate and its expansion, occasioned the Lorraine Primary school to be built there in 1957, and the Cordwalles Infants and Junior schools in 1961. Three years later Barossa Secondary Modern was built, followed by Pine Ridge First school. In Ballard Road the original Cordwalles School, a private Preparatory School that had existed there prior to World War II and had been used as a driving instruction school for the A.T.S. during the war, was later taken over by Collingwood School and utilised to house some of its sixth form pupils.

Meanwhile, the residential expansion of Camberley in the private-housing building sector between London Road and the Chobham/Bisley Roads had been rapidly getting under way between 1960 and 1970 and highlighted the need for schools in this location. In 1966, Prior Heath Primary School was built near Ravenswood Cross-roads and, in 1969, the "Graitney" estate became the site of Crawley Ridge Primary. In 1964, "Carwarden House" was acquired and a Special School for Children established there.

The last large estate built in Camberley's private housing area was at Heatherside where, starting in 1967, the Heather Ridge Primary, Middle and Secondary Schools were built to serve this neighbourhood.

In 1971, Surrey Education Authority re-organised education in this area on the basis of First, Middle and Comprehensive Schools. This led to the establishment of Collingwood School, which was an amalgamation of 3 existing schools, the old Camberley Grammar School, Barossa Secondary School and Bagshot Secondary School. France Hill Secondary Modern School then became a Comprehensive school as well. In Frimley, as the residential areas close to the village expanded, Tomlinscote Comprehensive School was built by the side of the old "Alphington" estate and Ravenscote Middle School in the grounds of the "Edmonscote" estate.

Further residential building is at present being thrust upon our Borough of Surrey Heath by the County Council. Perhaps few people fully realise the problems that this brings upon our own Council in respect of schools for the new inhabitants. The <u>County</u> Council has to provide these and is not always quick to do so, which results in a time lag between "need" and "fulfilment" as building programmes progress and new housing developments occur.

I hope that this chapter will serve to give my readers some idea of the number and variety of schools which become necessary as a town's population expands. Now that the Borough of Surrey Heath, which is double the size of the old Frimley and Camberley U.D.C., serves Chobham, Windlesham, Bagshot, Lightwater and West End as well, all expanding too, one can appreciate the difficulties in this respect that will have to be faced in the days to come and add a realisation of what this aspect of population expansion brings in its wake.

CHAPTER 31

Perhaps no book on Camberley which deals not only with houses and factories, but with people as well, would be quite complete without mention of three personalities who have in the present era made their way from small beginnings within our Frimley Manor to become widely known and highly successful entrepreneurs.

To tell you about them I have to rely upon my own memories and if these are not entirely accurate I must ask the three gentlemen of whom I am about to write to forgive me.

Just after World War II two brothers, of whom David Wickens was one, set up a large tent on a field in Frimley near to the railway and Hawley Lane. They had the brilliant idea of providing an auction market where the many surplus Army vehicles that were becoming available could be bought and sold. The auctioneers took a set commission on the sale. Soon they started to auction cars and commercial vehicles as well on the same basis, and car dealers found this a very useful means of quickly disposing of cars that they had taken in part exchange whilst selling a client a new car. Prospective buyers were given the opportunity to inspect vehicles the previous day to each weekly sale and many found good bargains here. It was not very long before a restaurant was built on the site, and this was not of the "lorry drivers pull-in" variety, but a well run and nicely decorated steak-house that was open in the evenings as well as in the day time for "family" usage. This was the start of the British Car Auction Company, now a world-wide concern with interests both here and in America. I believe that Mr David Wickens, no mean golfer I may add, is still at the head of the firm who have now moved their Auctioneering Establishment to Blackbushe Airport, whilst their old site in Frimley has become Frimley Business Park.

Charles Church, who has built so many of the houses in Camberley, was once the pupil of an old friend of mine, Cyril Matthews, who was the Headmaster of Windlesham School. He often spoke to me with pride of the attainments of his old scholar who had worked his way up from scratch to create the great building firm of which he is the head today. I have been much impressed by Mr Church's adherence to a single idea and theme. He has selected one market for his houses and stuck to this throughout. This has been the provision of "up-market" houses with particular attention to their exterior elevations. He has spurned very modernistic lines for these but instead maintained a policy of utilising the gracious design of Georgian and Tudor houses for the majority of his housing developments. Moreover, he invariably selects very appropriate sites for these in Southern England. His offices now occupy a large site in Knoll Road and he has a commercial development under way in Yorktown. As this area is obviously the probable target for re-development within the next few years, I trust that we may have buildings here that will be in keeping with their close proximity to the R.M.A. Sandhurst, which is of Georgian character.

The third of my Frimley Manor entrepreneurs is Bob Potter of the Lakeside Country Club. Before World War II, I remember Bob Potter's 3-piece band to which I sometimes danced - and also his music shop which was, I think, in Mytchett. Soon he had 9 Dance Bands on the road and then went in to the Dance Hall business but, with their decline, he looked for other ventures in the entertainment world. From this has come the "Show Biz" whizz-kid who now has Royalty attending his charity shows at Lakeside; and

Mrs Thatcher arriving to speak at the Small Business Conferences also held there. As well as staging the dining floor-shows featuring all our well-known variety celebrities, Lakeside also provides facilities for local organisations, such as the Probus Club, to hold monthly luncheon meetings in their Canal Suite. Just recently he has started to build a hotel, part of which extends over the Wharfenden Lake, an offshoot from the adjacent Basingstoke Canal. Is it a coincidence that this Lakeside property was once owned by Sir George Branson, the grandfather of another great Show Bizz personality, Richard Branson of Virgin Records and Virgin Airways fame!

Perhaps there are other entrepreneurs in Camberley of whom I am unaware. If so, my apologies for not including them in this Chapter. Maybe someone else will up-date this book in ten year's time as Camberley keeps on growing and then they will be able to put this right!

Selling your car?

The Southern Counties way is simple, quick and fair

Only 10/- entry fee. Commission if sold, 5% (minimum £5, maximum £25).
No sale—no commission!
Place your own reserve

AUCTIONS START AT 12 NOON AT
CHICHESTER every TUESDAY
FARNBOROUGH every WEDNESDAY
ALEXANDRA PALACE every THURSDAY

For full details and brochure write to:—

SOUTHERN COUNTIES CAR AUCTIONS LTD.

Alexandra Palace, London, N.22 (Tudor 5675) or Redskin Roundabout, Chichester By-Pass, Sussex (Chichester 3315) or Frimley Bridges, Farnborough, Hants. (Camberley 1544).

Early advertisement of the firm that became British Car Auctions.

Charles Church houses built on Chatsworth Heights, Colling Ridge.

H.R.H. Prince Charles has an informal chat with Mike Yarwood, Jack Solomons and Bob Potter at the Lakeside Country Club.

Camberley in 1986
and Camberley's Neighbours Developments

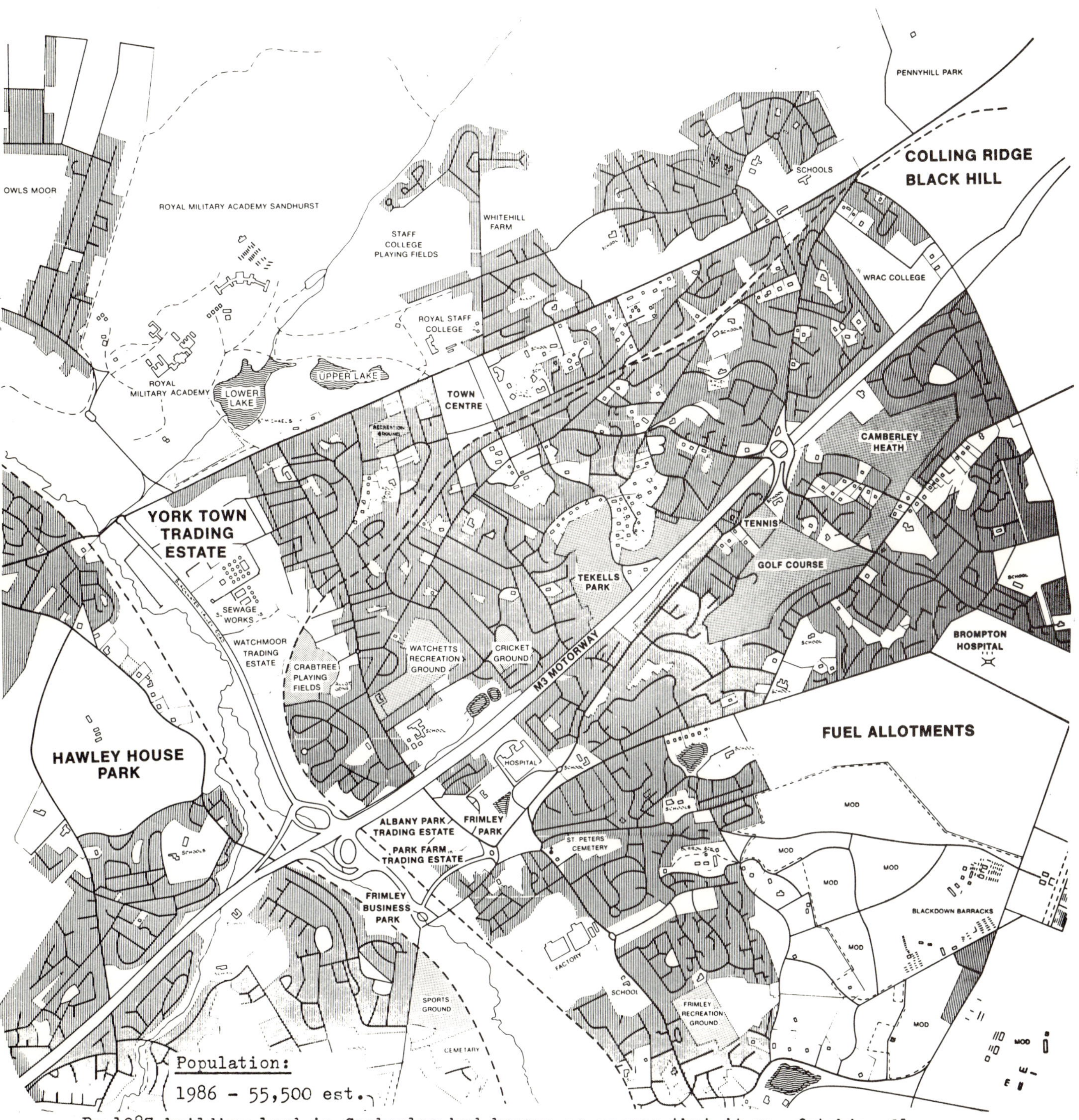

Population:
1986 - 55,500 est.

By 1987 building land in Camberley had become so scarce that it was fetching £1m. an acre and the fear of serious overcrowding had become a matter of great concern . Half of Brompton Hospital's grounds were sold to form Cheylesmore Park Estate and this just left the W.R.A.C. College grounds as the only other possible building site of any appreciable size that was as yet undeveloped. The only open "breathing spaces" that Camberley now has are Tekells Park,Camberley Heath Golf Course,Frimley Fuel Allotment, five Recreation Playing Fields and the fields possessed by the Schools. The Blackwater Valley Road has been constructed through the Industrial Area by the river and the Watchmoor Estate built there. Meanwhile Blackwater,Owlsmoor,Hawley and Farnborough have all been considerably built up. Hawley House Park is the only open site adjacent to Camberley,other than the Army lands that still surround us, that still retains it's original beauty. Long may the Ministry of Defence who control the Army lands still look upon this area as one suitable for their training purposes.

CHAPTER 32

As Camberley's residential area became almost completely built up, the private-housing Development Companies turned to Frimley and to the villages immediately surrounding the Manor, Blackwater, Lightwater, Yateley and Hawley, for further building land.

To the south of the Chobham/Bisley Road the old tenant farms of the Lord of Frimley Manor were situated along each side of the Frimley Green Road, two of which had been bought for Council House building estates. Balmoral Drive, a road constructed along Middle Moor, divided these two estates and in 1965 Johnsons Wax factory had been built at the end of this road close to the Blackwater River. Private-housing developers now constructed two more estates immediately to the east of the Ansell and Worsley estates. Just to the north of the former, the Alphington, and part of the Athallan estates were turned into the Tomlinscote Housing estate, and a County Secondary School built on the site of "Tomlinscote House" and a portion of the Fuel Allotments. One of the new housing estates was built around what had previously been the Burrow Hill T.B. Sanatorium Colony (now a school) and the other abutted St.Catherines, the Pain family's old home.

Middle Farm, Cross Farm and Bowling Green Farm, which lay to the south nearer to Frimley Green, were also developed about this time, a part of Middle Farm becoming a Council-owned Recreation Ground. To the east of St.Catherines, which has been developed with some pleasant houses, there is a large area of heathland stretching as far as the Deepcut Bridge Road. Four large houses, each with a considerable estate, lie hidden in the extreme western part of the heath. The rest contains the Frith Hill Reservoir and is used by the Army for training purposes, the soldiers being housed in the Deepcut Barracks, built around 1900, on land allocated to James Laurell and John Giles in 1801.

Just over our borders into Berkshire and Hampshire, very considerable developments have taken place in Sandhurst, Blackwater, Yateley, Hawley and Cove since World War II. Unfortunately for these rural communities, with the exception of Hawley, their farmlands were not held in just a few strong hands, as was the case in the Manor of Frimley, but in many different ones instead, and this has meant that developments there have occurred piece-meal, largely without much cohesion between the design of one group of buildings with those adjacent. Although their Parish Councils have done their best to try to exercise some control over this, they have been much handicapped by the fact that they are situated at the very extremity of their County boundaries and, until very recently, it seemed that their County Councils had little interest in these villages, so far away from their County centres. (Map, Page 123)

However, this has now altered, for just to the north of Blackwater, where the Wish Stream joins the river, three giant "High Street" firms, Sainsburys, Marks and Spencers and Tescos, are battling for the triangle of land which was once the farm fields of the Tekells' original Sandhurst Park Estate, sold to the Army for the foundation of the Royal Military College. Upon this, these firms wish to establish an "out of town" shopping centre which, if planning permission is eventually granted, will undoubtedly add very considerably to the already much overstretched traffic problems that confront us on all of Camberley and District's roads today. It will also possibly affect the commercial viability of shops in our Town Centre and those of our neighbours.

In Hampshire, the villages of Hawley and Blackwater have not suffered quite so much from piece-meal development as has Yateley. This is because there were 7 considerable land-owners with large estates in this area, thus affording a certain amount of continuity in the development of these estates as they have come upon the market.

Frogmore Park, on which Frogmore Park Drive and Rosemary Gardens now stand, was previously owned by Admiral Sir Charles Denniston Burney who, amongst other attainments, was an inventor. He helped in the designing of the airship R101 and also invented the paravane, used for mine-sweeping by the Navy, which brought him a large fortune. Another of his inventions was a rain-maker, and he sold the patent for this to someone in Rhodesia.

"Minley Manor", erected in 1858 by Mr Raikes Currie, remained in the possession of the family until it was taken over by the Army in World War II. The Manor House is still intact and the estate, situated on Hartford Bridge Flats, has not been built upon. "Starveacre", which lies on the common land between "Minley Manor" and "Hawley Hill House" (Hawley Hotel), has now been developed with middle-market houses by Bryant Homes Ltd., and the Hotel demolished and an estate built there by the Charles Church Co.

One of the most beautiful areas that still remains in our district is "Hawley Park". If you stand in the Watchetts Recreation Ground on a summer's day and look across the Blackwater River Valley to the Hartford Bridge Flats on the other side of the river, the Park can be seen. The House, which is now divided into flats, is hidden amongst trees, but the farmhouse and farmlands and the old stables belonging to Hawley Park are in use as an Equitation Centre. Squire Norris, who built our Obelisk in Camberley, once lived here, as did the Palmers (of Huntley and Palmer biscuit fame) before they moved to "Hawley Hill House". Today it is owned by the Spears family, the Camberley building firm. What a joy it would be to all of us who live on the borders of the three counties if our 3 County Councils could get together and purchase this beautiful unspoilt estate for use as a public park, if it were ever to come on to the open market.

Nearby is "Hawley Place", formerly called "Firbanks", and now a private school. This was once the home of Lord Revelstoke, a friend of King George V and Queen Mary. Princess Mary and her husband, Viscount Lascelles, spent a fortnight of their honeymoon there in 1922. Adjoining and surrounding "Hawley Place" was a Peat Moor in which is Hawley Lake. The Army owns this land, but the public have virtually unrestricted access to it and it is a favourite "open" area in Hawley much used by all who live in the village.

"Fernhill House" is not far away, in Fernhill Lane. Built in 1845 by Mr John Scovel, it was afterwards occupied by Sir Charles Pressley, who assisted Mr Gladstone to prepare his Budgets when he was Chancellor of the Exchequer. The house was sold in 1933 and became the home for Basque children refugees from the Spanish Civil War. In World War II it was commandeered by the Army and its beautiful interior desecrated. Shortly after the war, Southern Instruments (of whom I have spoken in Chapter 25) bought the house and started their firm up there. Fernhill Close is now built on the site of the house and other roads are in the grounds.

"Hawley Grange", further to the south, now has a Council housing estate built upon the surrounding farmlands, and from here to Hawley Lane is now one long sprawl of houses with factories along Hawley Lane.

The pressure put upon our Council after we became Surrey Heath Borough, and Bagshot, Windlesham and Chobham came within our boundaries, has been such that the demand for still more land for housing development has been the means of considerably altering the character of the two villages of Lightwater and West End. Mr Frederick Street started a Nursery Garden in West End after he left Heatherside in 1917, and just recently this has been removed to Arborfield and the land utilised for a housing estate. Along the Redroad Hill Road, as one nears its junction with the A322, there has been a large residential development and the Lightwater Country Park provides recreational facilities nearby.

Another new recreational centre now being made between Frimley Green and Mytchett in the fields that belonged to Frimley Lodge is situated in the triangle bordered by the railway, Basingstoke Canal and Mytchett Road. When completed, there is to be a 9-hole pitch and putt course in addition to playing fields, and the Canal is to be utilised for water sports which will include canoeing. A project is also afoot to clean up the Blackwater River valleyside, which has been used as a dumping ground for all sorts of refuse by contractors for many years, especially near Ash. Riverside walks are being made and the gravel pit lakes that abound between Sandhurst and Frimley Green are being stocked with fish. The tri-lakes area near Sandhurst has, of course, been used for some time in this way.

The industrial development of Bristow Farm continues at high speed. The Blackwater Valley Road has been made to join Blackwater to Frimley, going through both Bristow and Park Farms, and it is proposed to continue this onwards both northwards and southwards parallel to the river. This has also done something towards relieving the increasing traffic problems that were being experienced by heavy vehicles entering the Yorktown Industrial Estate from Frimley Road. Already there have been many additional industrial factories built at the Blackwater end of the new road, and now its central portion designated "The Watchmoor Industrial Estate" is in the course of construction. At the southern end, near to the M3 entrance, is the "Frimley Business Park" which, together with "Albany Park", situated between Park Farm and the Motorway, has many new factories. At the back of the "Tippex" factory in Admiralty Way, the Blackwater River walk starts and the old bridge can be seen from here exactly as it used to look 180 years ago. The new carriageway which has been built over the top of it to carry the London Road and the railway is almost invisible from the towpath.

The strip of land that lies to the immediate south of Watchmoor Industrial Estate is to become another recreational facility, according to the present plan. It would be nice to see this made into a garden area, with rock gardens and waterfalls set amongst flower beds, to make a break between the Estate and the river.

At this point in time, 1987, all of what was once the waste lands of Frimley Heath, first enclosed by James Laurell in 1801, has been turned into a vast housing estate with only 3 open spaces left within it, Tekells Park, Camberley Heath Golf Course and the Royal Albert Orphanage/W.R.A.C. College Estate. A planning application to build 400 houses on the latter estate is now being considered and will, in all probability, be looked upon favourably by our Council. A move is also afoot that might result in the sale of the Golf Course to outside interests. Tekells Park is, however, in the firm hands of the Theosophists. But, in the end, it is only our Council who can make sure that at least the latter two "breathing spaces" are preserved within what is now a completely built-up residential area. They have shown a thoroughly commendable resolve to preserve Frimley's vital open space, the Fuel Allotments, from building. One hopes that they will not falter in this, and that the heritage that belongs to all of Frimley Manor's present day inhabitants will be passed on intact for further generations to enjoy.

POPULATION FIGURES

District	1841 Population	1841 Houses	1981 Population	1981 Houses
Camberley (North of Chobham/Bisley Road)	804	175	35,208	11,546
Frimley (Southwards to Middle Farm)	315	62	6,005	1,986
Frimley Green - (Previously South End) (Southwards to the Railway)	318	76	5,678	1,795
Mytchett (Southwards 1 mile to Ash)	98	21	4,517	1,616
All population figures quoted in this book are those applicable to the original Frimley and Camberley U.D.C. which comprised the above. (Refer Maps, Pages 15,29 and 134)	1,535	334	51,408	16,943

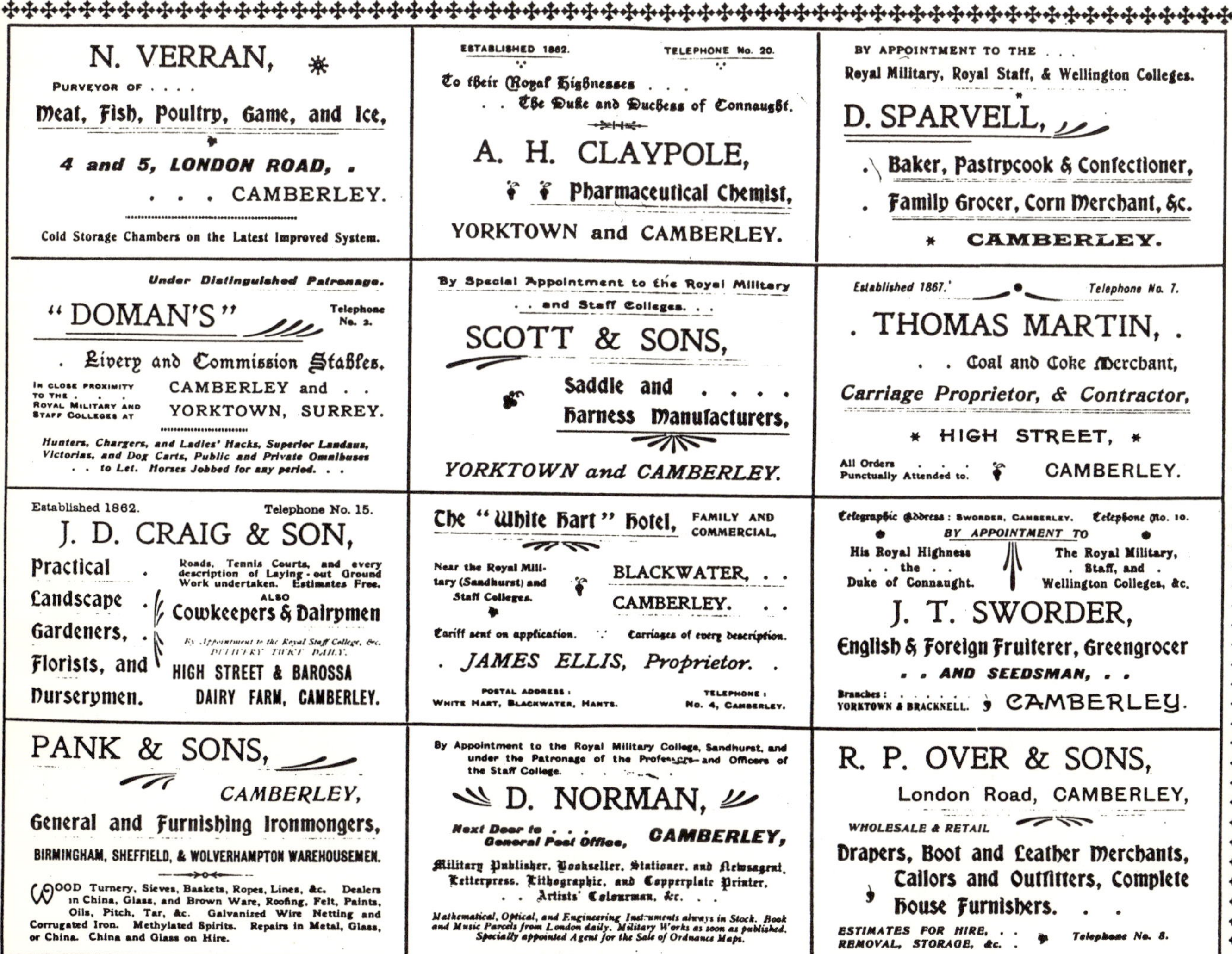

Advertisements in an 1898 brochure

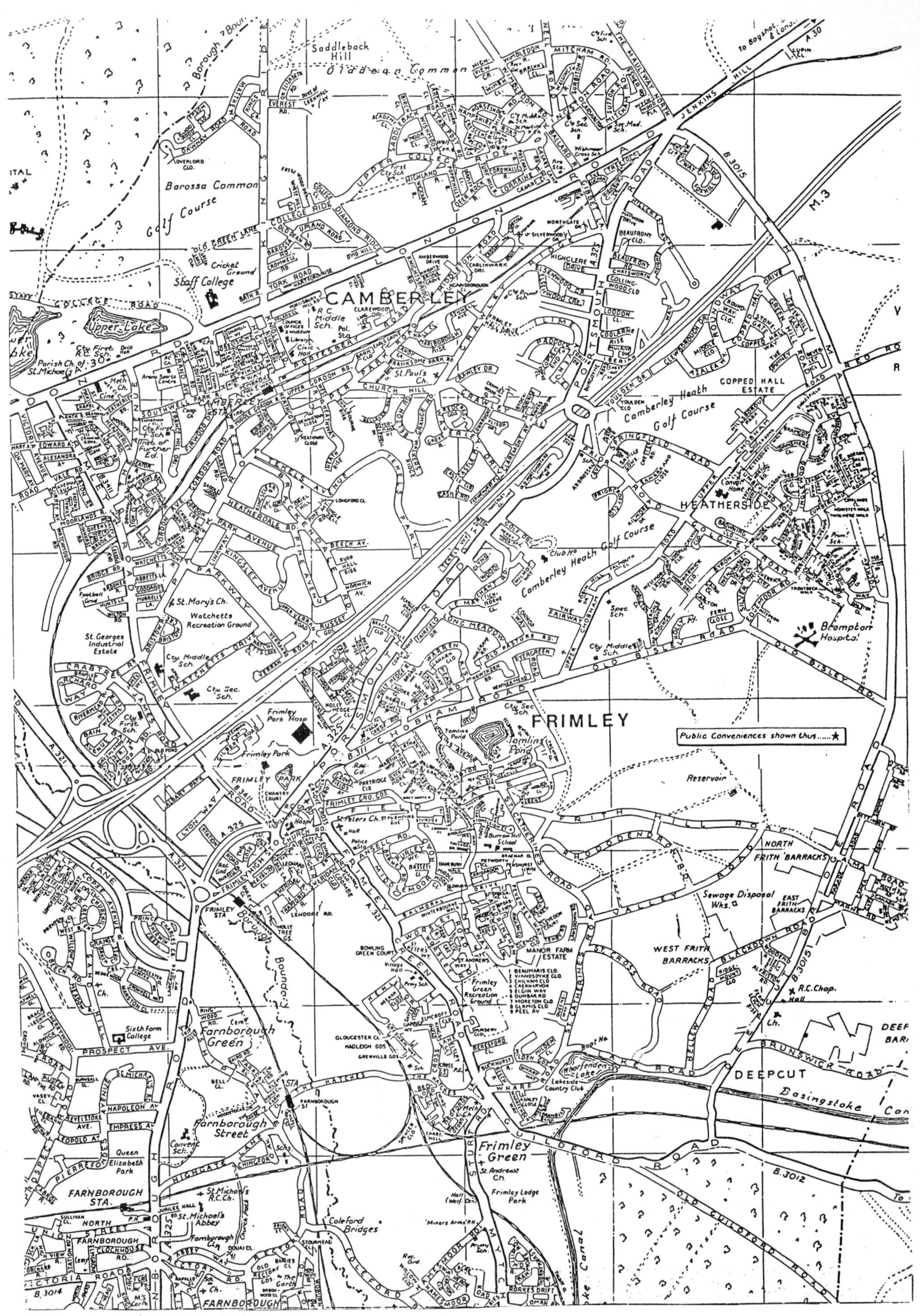

"Map by courtesy of G.I.Barnett & Son Ltd."